PAYTHAN

PAYTHAN

— A Novel By —

Kim Marie & Christopher Knopf

PAYTHAN

ISBN: 979-8-9875171-0-9 (paperback)

ISBN: 979-8-9875171-1-6 (ebook)

First published by Mirror Dog, January 2023

MIRROR DOG

Cover & Layout by Mary Wright

Dedication

In dedication to a man who has set the bar higher than anyone I know. You have touched lives in the ninety-one years you were with us and you continue to do so even though you moved on. Thank you, Chris and Lorraine, for all you have blessed us all with over the years.

To all the women and children who have been exploited and forced into human slavery, and for those not found. They will never be forgotten.

Chris, his wife Lorraine, and Kim

Table of Contents

Acknowledgments

I am honored to have been asked to write *Paythan*.

I was asked to write Paythan after my writing mentor Chris, who started the story, passed away after writing about a fifth of the manuscript. Someone said to me soon after: "The mentor is still mentoring his student even when he isn't physically here."

That ignited something deep inside my soul. It sounds like something Chris would do after my last visit with him. At that time he had fallen ill, little did I know it would be the last time I would see him. He wrote a little note in one of his books to me before I left that day. It said, "I'm passing the torch to you kid."

At his celebration of life, we were blessed to see the incredible impact he had on so many lives, from his children and grandchildren to friends, students and extended family. He and his wife, Lorraine, truly lived in their purpose together. They touched many lives in their work and through the incredible, gracious love, respect and support they gave to those special relationships. They set the bar higher than most could live up to. Each person had a consistent "take away" from Chris. He taught all the women in his life what a gentle, kind, supportive, strong, and compassionate man looks like and he taught the same to the men in his life. As many others, I respected Chris and Lorraine's incredible relationship. That became the measuring stick in my own life and in the relationships I have built. This incredible couple set the example we would all strive to have in building our own relationships.

I wouldn't be where I am today in my writing skills if it hadn't been for Chris. His mentorship and encouragement gave me the courage to move forward. It was relationships with people like Chris that have taught me over the years how important mentors are. Seniors that have life experience and stories to pass down their wisdom and experiences, and teach all of us. I will always cherish this special relationship that has helped me grow as an individual. When Lorraine asked me to take over writing where Chris left off, I was honored and scared. How could I possibly live up to one of the most admired men I had ever had in my life? When she shared the sixty pages or so that he had written I realized there was so much more to this story, and my soul knew that I could help bring this story to life. I could tell this story with a deeper meaning and purpose.

For many years I have worked with the Native American community, and it was important to me to honor Chris and the story of this young Native American man who was a former student of Chris' at USC. I asked Lorraine if I could take the story in a different direction and dedicate the story to the Murdered and Missing (MMIW), bringing awareness to human trafficking, to issues many avoid talking about. She instantly said "yes," and she felt that Chris would have supported and loved what I wanted to do with the story.

Immediately, I set out calling on friends who led me from one person to the next to help me uncover truth. True stories were shared from victims/survivors of trafficking, judges, US Marshals, FBI, law enforcement, hospitals, social services, elders from reservations and so many others that participated, helping to give a voice to the voiceless. In collaboration with these incredible people, I continued where Chris left off, collectively bringing together these stories to share what became Paythan. Lorraine and I were able to spend quality time together in honor of Chris. Her personal stories, guidance and support were incredible as I brought this to life. It is the journey that brings the most impact.

My hope is to awaken, to educate, to shift people's perspectives to take action. Most importantly, I hope to bring people together from all cultures and races. This epidemic does not see gender, color, or race. There is a common thread to this sickness and there is a common thread to the solution. Together we can unravel it and heal. Together we can make the shift, to change and save lives.

Isolating from one another will not make change and it will not stop the discrimination. It will not stop the countless murders, it will not stop domestic violence, it will not stop suicide, or mental health issues. I would like to give a friendly reminder to younger women and men to respect and appreciate the elders in their lives. Remind everyone that the elders in our world deserve the respect they have been earning over their years. They are an incredible source to learn from in benefiting your profession, walking your spiritual journey, in building your relationships and enjoying the pleasures of life.

Who would have known that this incredible journey would bring me to this very moment? That twenty years ago when I moved to Los Angeles, not knowing a soul, I would be blessed to have met Chris, be invited to study with him and work from his home, to be included in his extended family and get to know their beautiful life together.

This is a magnificent (wonderful, marvelous, spectacular) example of how impactful mentorship can be and how valuable our senior community is to learn from and help us grow into people that can be strong enough, worthy enough and humble enough to receive the torch when it is passed down. Not only receive it, but respect whom it came from and respect taking that knowledge and wisdom bestowed to honor it and evolve it to the next level.

Thank you, Chris, for your guidance and mentorship. Thank you to everyone who has divinely come into my life to help bring this project to print and into the lives of those who are open and ready to receive. There is a common thread weaving throughout. This was truly a community project and could not be possible without everyone who participated.

Please, if you need help, if you are alone, if you are feeling depressed, if you do not feel safe in your relationship, there is help in every community. You can reach out and there will be someone there to help. Please see the end of the book or go to our website www.mirrordog.com to find some national references for help. There is always a way out. God is protecting you and if you are reading this, it may just be a divine message to help shift you into the direction where you will find your purpose and peace. Thank you for your support and reading our story.

In Light, Love and Gratitude,

Kim Marie

Waŋží

1

The historic highway seemed desolate for only a moment before the sound of a motorcycle engine replaced the gentle whisper of wind amongst the sea of long golden wheat grass on rolling hills. The blue sky filled with billowing white clouds, telling a story with no end in sight. A black Moto Guzzi Stone motorcycle passed a sign in a blur, going over a hundred miles per hour on Highway 16.

Moments later, the motorcycle pulled up to a small rural stand-alone gas station that appeared to have been there for decades, the sign rusted and weathered. At the pump, a young man wearing a black leather jacket, jeans, and black boots removed his helmet, revealing long, flowing black hair. He dismounted and unzipped his jacket, revealing a tight white tank top, exposing his defined abs. Paythan, a young Lakota American Indian on break from USC, looked at his cell phone, finding a message from his sister Aiyana. She included a picture of two young women smiling, sitting inside a vehicle, being photobombed by a young man and woman sitting behind them.

Aiyana's message read, *"Hey bro, hurry up! We are almost there! Where are you? We can't wait to see you!"*

Paythan typed back, *"On my way, few more hours, got a late start."*

He returned the nozzle to the pump and walked toward the store, still texting on his phone.

A bright red Silverado pickup truck occupied by two White men with shaved heads recklessly skidded up to a pump, blaring country music. As the driver stepped out of the truck, he flicked his cigarette onto the ground and crushed it with his combat boot, staining the pavement with tobacco. He glared as the door closed behind the young man walking into the gas station. The driver walked to the open window to talk to the passenger. As he leaned into the window, his shirt lifted, revealing the butt of a Glock 19 handgun. The interior of the truck was dusty, with ammo boxes on the middle console, a pack of cigarettes, a bottle filled with discarded chew in one of the cup holders, and a large can of Miller Lite beer in the other. In the back seat were a couple of ballistic vests, what appeared to be a rifle of some sort, and a duffle bag.

Paythan, returning to his motorcycle, did not notice the hairless man standing by the pickup, glaring at him. He started to pack the jerky and energy drink he just purchased into his bag, and then put on his helmet. He heard crude words coming from the man on the other side of the pump.

"Hey, Pocahontas. We can give you a real haircut."

Paythan ignored him and started his motorcycle, only angering the skinhead, who yelled over the revving of the motorcycle engine, "Hey, red nigger, I'm talking to you!" The man stepped closer to the rear of the bike as it quickly sped off.

***

A white passenger van came to a slow, rolling stop as it approached protestors standing on top of similar white non-descriptive vans, blocking the highway to Mount Rushmore. There were hundreds of men and women gathered around, some wearing a form of red, while some covered their mouths with a red handprint. The closer they got, the louder the chanting became, "Save our land and stand with us!"

In the window of the van, a vibrant young Native American girl watched the crowds in front of her. Her long, shiny, dark brown hair blew in her face. As she brushed it away, her soulful brown eyes with flakes of amber revealed a window to her gentle soul. Aiyana turned to her friend.

"Dakota, I'm a little nervous. What if we get arrested? We hardly know these guys." She looked around the van.

"You worry too much. It will be great!"

"Maybe we should wait for my brother. They're his friends."

"Paythan said he is hours away. Look, we're here! You said you wanted to be a voice for the missing girls. The press is here. We have a chance to get the word out."

Dakota and Aiyana had been best friends since they were six years old, growing up on the Pine Ridge Reservation in South Dakota. Dakota had always been the instigator and had a knack for being able to talk Aiyana into doing just about anything.

Aiyana was soft-spoken - *pure of heart* they called her - always wanting to save everyone and everything. Her smile could light up the darkest of places, and her passion and genuineness radiated through those deep, soulful eyes.

One of the men in the front turned to the girls. "Our ancestors would be proud we still are fighting for rights and our sacred land." He couldn't have sounded any more arrogant.

Dakota snapped back, "What about our missing sisters? Wouldn't our ancestors be proud we are fighting for them?"

The man rolled his eyes. "Who invited her?" he grumbled to the driver.

Aiyana grabbed Dakota's arm and pulled her back down in her seat. "Please don't start with him. Save it for out there."

Outside, the crowd seemed to be growing. Aiyana and her friends joined the peaceful protestors. The girls got caught up in the excitement and found themselves being swept away in the crowd of people who seemed to be following whoever was leading. The protestors began to cheer and chant louder and louder, taking the girls farther and farther from the van. As they moved closer to the front of the crowd, they could see chaos starting.

The National Guard was fully armed, dispersing pepper spray, gas bombs, and rubber bullets, trying to force the protestors to recede, yelling "Move, move, move!"

The protestors continued their advance and continued chanting, causing the National Guard to retreat.

Off in the distance, a reporter started a newscast about the protest as a fight to recover the Black Hills, put a stop to the man camps from the big oil companies, and to bring awareness for missing indigenous women. The Black Hills had been taken over by the government. The tribes were trying to put a stop to the man camps because they increased crimes, especially against women. Even when the man camps left, the impact on the community remained. It didn't only affect the reservations, but also the local farmers who dug wells for the cattle and other farmers. The man camps took up a minimum of eighty acres and would deplete the local water sources.

Reporters knew they had a short window before their stories would be blacked out of the mass media machine, which was usually what happened to any stories regarding Native Americans. They tried to get the best angles of the demonstration and made attempts to interview some of the protestors. A native woman stood waiting for her interview, the crowd behind her chanting, holding up their signs. The reporter, ready to go live, motioned to the woman to come closer.

"We go live in thirty seconds."

The woman nodded; they stood waiting for the countdown.

"Thank you, John. I'm Sara Abraham, reporting live from the protest at the Black Hills. Here with me today is Cheryl, a survivor of abuse and trafficking, to share her story after she was denied sharing her testimony by the board."

Cheryl began to graphically describe the bruises, bite marks, and the abuse she had endured after her first rape by a non-native man.

Aiyana and Dakota made their way towards the reporters, holding up their signs: STAND WITH US FOR THE MISSING OR THE MURDERED REAL MEN BEAT DRUMS NOT WOMEN.

Other signs emerged - PROTECT THE SACRED LAND - as chanting and singing echoed behind them. They were determined to get noticed on camera and make it on the evening news.

The sun began to set, turning the blue sky a fiery orange, and the grassy knoll filled with more protestors and bystanders. Indians on horses with red handprints painted on them marched down the highway. The more the crowd grew, other protestors were counter-protesting the protestors.

The white supremacists started to move in, holding their signs, disagreeing with the protest. They were yelling out "Go home and get drunk and leave us alone!"

The protestors had had enough of the harassment. They moved their protests across the road and formed a tighter barricade, preventing any more from entering. Indigenous women and children led the blockade across the road, carrying their signs and chanting, "Land back for the missing and murdered women!"

The National Guard, failing to keep the crowd back, was reinforced by local law enforcement. As the police force grew, the protestors could not hold them off much longer. Suddenly, what had been a peaceful protest had begun to turn hostile as law enforcement came in full force to break up the protestors. The news media shut off all cameras and headed back to their vehicles, no longer covering the massive attack on the protestors. This was no surprise, as the media has been instructed not to cover the attacks by government on the protestors. They were known to twist the stories, as if the protestors were the ones causing the riots, when they were only protecting themselves from the malicious attacks ordered by the powers-that-be, keeping the masses in the dark.

As the crowd turned into a stampede, tow trucks were brought in to remove the vehicles that were blocking the highway. People were getting arrested. Aiyana and Dakota scrambled to find their friends, having to dodge the skinheads who were causing fights among each other and the protestors. It seemed that almost everyone was out for themselves, causing chaos and making it difficult for them to get through the crowd.

Paythan had been shut out by one of many roadblocks. He tried to break through the barriers, only for officers to threaten him and push him back. Worried about Aiyana, he had tried texting and calling her, but his phone had no service.

Aiyana and Dakota tried to make it back to their van. Aiyana, feeling overwhelmed, with tears filling her eyes, looked at Dakota and held up her phone. "I don't have service. What are we going to do?"

Dakota saw the driver from the van. "There's Chayton. Let's go." The girls ran to him. He was distraught as he tried to find a way out of the crowd. "Follow me."

He grabbed Dakota by the wrist and she grabbed Aiyana. They pushed their way through the crowd, Aiyana still trying to text Paythan. Chayton found a couple of the others from the van; they yelled back and forth at one another, trying to figure a way out.

"Let's go! Just get to the van, it's over here."

The other two men started to walk away. "We are staying, catch up with you later."

***

The dark, two-lane highway was only lit by the headlights of the van. Chayton, nervously looking in the rear-view mirror, said, "That was amazing! I didn't think we were going to get out of there. Did you see those guys tearing each other apart?"

Banter started amongst the friends as they replayed the event. Aiyana, distracted and still trying to text Paythan, got service for a moment sent out a text. "Where are you?"

Paythan had made it back to the hotel, and was sitting in bed with his laptop open, reading an email from his college professor. It was giving him instructions on how to submit his screenplay. His phone chirped. He saw Aiyana's message.

He replied, "I'm at the hotel. How long before you get here? I'm in room 222."

He waited for her response. It seemed like an eternity before she messaged him back. "I'm not sure, Chayton is driving, he said we are almost out of gas. He needs to stop."

"Text me when you get closer."

***

The van pulled into a newer and very busy gas station with a big M on the sign. Chayton got out to pump the gas while Dakota and Kay decided to go in for snacks and to use the restroom. He called out to his girlfriend, "Kay, get me a Dew!"

Aiyana stayed in the van for a few minutes, looking out the window and watching her friends, then she decided to run into the store with them. A truck of skinheads pulled in, making a scene. Chayton got back in the van. He wondered what was taking the others so long.

Kay walked towards the van. The skinheads were staring, and one with a mohawk began making rude comments. Chayton couldn't hear, so he got out of the van. "Kay, come on!"

Skinheads yelled out to her, "Hey Squaw, five bucks for a b.j! Hey, we're talking to you!"

She walked faster and quickly got into the van. They tried to wait for the other girls to come out, but the skinheads started to walk toward the van, one carrying a baseball bat, while the other had a gun in his waistband. Chayton put the van in drive. Kay yelled at him, "You have to wait for Dakota and Aiyana! They're coming!"

"They'll be fine! Text them to wait inside, and we'll come back for them."

The skinheads got closer and Chayton pulled out so fast that the wheels spun. Accelerating too quickly, he fishtailed. Two of the skinheads ran back to their truck and took off after them.

***

Back at the motel, Paythan was still on his computer, working on his screenplay for his professor when his phone went off and a text came through from Aiyana. *"Chayton took off. Left Dakota and me at the gas station. My battery is low."*

Paythan typed back, *"Wait there."*

He tried to call Chayton, but there was no answer. He had started to pace, looking at his phone, when headlights flashed through his window. Chayton, one of Paythan's closest childhood friends, pulled into the parking lot. Paythan ran out to meet them as they walked towards his room.

"Where's my sister, asshole?" He shoved Chayton.

Kay stepped between them while Chayton apologized. "I'm sorry man, they chased us. The girls are fine. We lost the assholes. Came to get you so we can go back and get them."

"Lost who?" He shoved him again. Kay moved between them again.

"Fucking skinheads came after us."

Frustrated, Paythan shoved Chayton towards the door. "Get in the van. Show me where they are."

Kay texted Aiyana to tell her they were on their way back.

As the van pulled into the gas station, it was just as busy, if not busier, than earlier. They scanned the area, looking for Aiyana and Dakota. Chayton kept an eye out for the skinheads, though it seemed that most of the gas station was full of them. Paythan looked around. "What the hell, it looks like a supremacists' reunion!"

Skinheads filled the area, many with their banners still up, indicating that they had been at the protest. He parked the van near the side of the building, as Paythan tried to call Aiyana, but it went to voicemail. Kay texted both girls to tell them where they were, and tried to call Dakota, but it went straight to voicemail.

Kay and Paythan looked around the area. Chayton was getting nervous, "Fuck man, let's get them and go. These guys will fuck us up." Paythan tried one more time to call Aiyana, but it kept going to voicemail.

"Chayton, you guys wait here. I'll go in and get them."

Kay started to follow Paythan out of the van. "Wait I'll go with you"

"No, stay with Chayton."

Paythan pulled his sweatshirt hood over his head, trying not to make eye contact with anyone. He was able to make it inside the gas station unnoticed. He walked around inside quickly, looking for the girls, but there was no sign of them. He thought to himself, *Maybe they're in the bathroom.* He knocked on the bathroom door, checking to see if anyone was watching him. Slowly opening the door, he yelled, "Aiyana, Dakota, let's go!"

No answer.

He stepped inside and announced; "Man in the room, ladies!" He was relieved that the bathroom was empty.

He found a red bandana in the end stall on the floor, like the one Aiyana was wearing in the picture she had sent him. He started to exit the restroom when a white woman, dressed in black and wearing combat boots, almost bumped into him. She started yelling, causing a scene, "Red nigger, what the fuck? Hey, there's an Indian in the women's bathroom!"

Paythan went to the clerk at the register, ignoring the woman. "Ma'am, I'm looking for my sister and her friend. They were here less than an hour ago." He showed her the picture they sent him earlier. The cashier watched the crowd start to gather behind Paythan.

"I've never seen them before. You need to leave. Now!"

Paythan refused to look behind him. "Not without my sister. They were here. Where did they go? You have cameras."

The cashier was getting nervous as several men were peering through the windows, waiting for Paythan to leave. "I never saw them. You need to leave. Leave now or I'm calling the police."

Paythan looked over his shoulder. "Yes, call the police. Call them! I'm not leaving without my sister."

The cashier watched as the seething woman from the bathroom joined the few men standing outside the gas station. The cashier leaned closer to Paythan and whispered, "The girls left with some guy in a blacked-out SUV. That's all I saw. But you need to leave before they come in here. Go out the back."

Paythan looked at who was waiting for him outside the doors. He stepped slowly away from the cashier and walked towards the back, making it appear as if he was going to the men's room, then made a run for the exit door, adjacent to it. The men out front split up. Two ran through the store behind him while the other attempted to cut him off behind the building.

He made it to the van, yelling, "Go, go!"

"Where are they?" Kay started to panic. Chayton started to drive as the men chased on foot after the van. Paythan tried to catch his breath. "They weren't there. I looked everywhere, and the cashier said they left in some guy's SUV. I found this in the bathroom."

Kay gasped, "Chayton! That's Aiyana's bandana…"

He cut her off. "They are fine. They probably got a ride from someone from the Res and are waiting at the hotel right now."

Back at the hotel, there was no sign of Aiyana or Dakota. Paythan opened the door to the room. "Chayton, they are not here. I'm going back."

"Maybe we should call the police."

Paythan grabbed a jacket and put his things back in his bag. "They won't come. I'm going. Come with me or don't, but I'm going."

"We will wait here in case they come."

Paythan shook his head, then shoved him out of the way.

"This is your fault, you asshole!"

Kay tried to grab Paythan by the wrist, but he pulled away, "Wait. We should at least try and call the police. Maybe I should go with you."

"No. Stay here and call me as soon as they get here. You can call the police, but I'm not waiting."

Paythan slammed the door behind him. Kay tried to call Dakota again, but it still went straight to voicemail.

Núŋpa

2

Four weeks had passed since Paythan left for break. It had been a bad day and was going to get worse, as Alan Fitzgerald had yet to discover as he sat in his car and watched them arrive in twos and threes, dressed in coats and ties that they hadn't worn since high school graduation.

The chapel, he found as he entered, was small for a university this size, and strictly nondenominational. Seating himself at the rear of the room, he looked about. There were twelve rows of seats, twenty to a row. There was a dais, but no altar, no glory windows or cross. It seemed more class-room than church. He looked up as a woman approached him.

"Mr. Fitzgerald?"

"Alan Fitzgerald, yes," he said.

"I'm Rabbi Geller, the university chaplain." She extended her hand. She was forty, he guessed, lean and professional, dressed in a black suit.

"I'll be speaking first, then I'll ask you to say some words. Following that, if you could encourage one or two in his fraternity to come forward? They'll be shy about that, but I understand they respect you."

Which was odd. He had never met anyone of them before, though he had spoken to two on the phone. Still, he nodded in agreement.

"We'll start in ten minutes," she said.

He watched her withdraw to the front of the chapel, encouraging the arrivals to occupy the front rows. He closed his eyes and reflected. It had already been not the best of days.

"Be in Mr. Ganz's office at 9:30 tomorrow morning," he had been informed by phone the day before. 9:30 Ganz, 2:30 the funeral service.

He slumped back in his chair, his mind going back to the beginning of the day. He had arrived at CBS' offices at Fairfax and Third promptly that morning, as requested, and immediately knew there was going to be trouble. Four months earlier, he had been summoned to write a movie for television that was being put into development based on a Sixty Minutes segment on the life of the infamous Nelson Carr. Carr controlled a political machine that dominated southeast Texas through graft, bribery, and fraud, and was rumored to have had political enemies murdered until his death by suicide. At the time, Alan had been assigned parking privileges alongside the building next to the executives' Mercedes and Teslas. This time he had been sent to Lot 2, a quarter-mile walk, it seemed, to the building entrance.

Paul Ganz's office was on the third floor. Already present were the producers, the Varner Brothers, two highly respected talents who had hired Alan, and were uncomfortably awaiting what was to come. The office was largely a mess from construction. A closet was being turned into a private bathroom, the traditional signature of success in Hollywood. A bar was being installed. Awards Ganz had earned, were in full display in a glass-fronted case.

A writer-producer who had worked his way up from series TV to some admittedly worthy long-form specials, Ganz was not a beloved man. His favorite recollection, which he liked to tell anyone who hadn't heard it, was the time he and his fourth wife were in a battle of words. Pounding him with every invective she could think of, she suddenly saw him bolt from his chair.

"Hold that!" he told her with seeming excitement, looking for pen and paper. "Great dialogue! Let me write that down!"

How Ganz had gotten the job heading the network Movie Division bewildered the writing community, who had generally worked well with his predecessor. Ganz wouldn't have the job long, Alan knew, but he had it now and he wasted no time exercising his authority.

When Alan had been asked to write the teleplay, he had accepted eagerly. He despised the manipulation of human beings for personal gratification and power and looked forward to portraying it through the life and chicanery of a genuinely despicable man. He had researched Carr thoroughly, research being his strong suit, and had come up with a script that delighted the Varners.

Not so fast. Difficult, mercurial, and dictatorial, Ganz was only remotely enthusiastic with the script as written and wanted massive changes. First, they couldn't use Carr's name, or the name of his state. Make it generic. Secondly, get rid of the wife, bring in a girl, let's say he'd kidnapped, and write in a rape. Further, add a State Ranger assigned to bring the girl out, and build up a love interest between the two when they meet.

Alan's stomach was churning. He stared at Ganz.

"A rape," he said. "Why?"

Alan didn't recall that Ganz gave a reasonable answer, he was too upset to recall much of anything. All he did recall was that Ganz wanted a rape. All eyes, the Varners' especially, were on Alan. Producers in the television world seldom received a dime until a script was ordered for production, unlike the writer, who was paid whether or not his script was usable. If Alan said no, these producers would receive nothing unless they could move the project ahead with somebody else. Alan hated what he was being told to do. It had no place in the story, and he told Ganz so. Further, Nelson Carr, especially as Alan had written him, would never have reduced himself to rape; it was beneath him. His magnetic personality and the fear and power he projected were such in Carr's mind that he would never have to.

What Alan hated most was Ganz's reason for demanding it. He was establishing his authority. Alan gave his reasons for opposing the requested rewrite and told Ganz that no, he couldn't do that. He was sorry, but no.

"How can we let a brother go?" Rabbi Geller was giving her eulogy. "How do we say, 'I'm ready now to go on without you?' How can we ever have a clue what that really means? And all of a sudden, the moment is upon us. And then we know what grief is."

She was finished and looked toward Alan. He rose, walked the length of the room to the lectern, and faced his audience. He was not a polished public speaker, but this was a must. There were twenty of them; he noticed ages of eighteen to twenty-two. He saw tears and heard an occasional sob. Death, he realized, was very different to the young. They had no preparation for it. He had lost a brother as a teenager, so he could empathize.

"Three years ago," he began, "the head of the screenwriting division here at the university asked me to take over a class. Advanced screenwriting. Twelve students. It always seemed to break down into four with talent following sample submissions to the department, four that wanted me to do all the work, and four you wondered how they got in."

It had been meant as a stab at humor. No laughter.

"One of the more extraordinary students I experienced," he went on, "came into class this past year. His name was Paythan Burke, a Lakota Indian off a South Dakota reservation, sent to the university by the tribal council, who paid his tuition and fraternity dues. He was in class one month and dropped out."

As he spoke, he saw a woman enter through the door at the back of the room. The sight was so striking that it gave him a moment's pause. In her mid-thirties, she was dressed in jeans, boots, and a light-colored shirt, her coal black hair cascading around a tawny-skinned oval face, full lips with no lipstick, and piercing black eyes. Getting past the moment, he continued.

"I was concerned about his departure, learned he was fighting alcohol and had dropped out to enter rehab. The following January, he reentered school, and by summer vacation, he had completed the first act of a startlingly compelling screenplay. Some years ago, when I'd written an episode for a TV show, the producer called me to come in. 'You didn't like it,' I said. 'Pretty words, kid,' he replied. 'But?' I said. 'Where are *you* in this?' he answered."

"It was something I always preached to my students," Alan went on. "Few got it. Paythan did. Though what he completed was only forty pages for the term, the story he was telling was filled with his soul. It was a dramatization of a Lakota legend of bravery over evil and twisted minds. School out, I got a call from one of his fraternity brothers, Hal Ward." Alan looked over the group in front of him. "Hal, are you here?"
A student, one from the gathering, half raised his hand in acknowledgment.

"Had I heard from Paythan? He wanted to know. I hadn't, I told him. Why would I? 'He thought a lot of you,' Hal told me, then said, 'He's disappeared. No one knows where he is.' A week later, he was found in a morgue in Tijuana. He'd gotten drunk, they said, was jaywalking, and was hit by a motorcycle."

It was the crux of the story, all of which they knew by now. He rambled on for another ten minutes, eulogizing Paythan with one cliché after another, trying to find his way to a conclusion and finally settling on asking if anyone would like to speak. Hal, with some reluctance, came forward and replaced Alan at the dais. Twice, the boy tried to overcome the grip in his throat. He couldn't.

Alan looked toward the rear of the chapel for the woman he had seen enter while he was speaking. She was gone.

***

Sunset Plaza Drive twisted and climbed its way up the mountain from Sunset Boulevard in West Hollywood. Alan had bought a house there three years earlier, a two-story, two bedroom modern on stilts perched above the canyon below. At the time, it was a choice of either the hills with its incredible view of the city, or the flat lands of Santa Monica.

"Incredible investment," the realtor had told him. "Prices in these hills are going to rocket."

They hadn't. Fear of fires and flood had kept prices stable, while Santa Monica was going through the roof. Still, it served Alan well. Living room and kitchen and dining area upstairs, the two bedrooms down, one of which he'd turned into an office.

Arriving home at five, Alan was taken by two things. The first was the Prius parked across the street, one house up, with a sticker on its rear windshield identifying it as a rental. Someone was seated inside it. The second was as he entered. The message light on his telephone was blinking an urgent red. The phone began to ring; he knew who it was before he answered the call.

"Yeah, Jer," he said when the party came on the line.

Jerry Loberg was Alan's long-time representative at William Morris. As an agent, he was meticulous at his job, but also a trickster. In negotiations with a network or studio head, he would always pick the hottest day.

"Let's take a walk," he'd say.

Down El Camino Drive to Olympic, left to Robertson, Jerry would lay out the terms of the deal for his client. His opposite would invariably start with a flat, "Ridiculous," but the sun and his lack of conditioning would soon be getting to him. His luxurious designer suit would become stained with sweat. Jerry, by contrast, in superb condition, was fully prepared to continue on to La Cienega 'til finally, the deal he was offering was beginning to sound better and better, if only Jerry would turn back.

"What's up?" Alan said into the phone.

"You walked out on Ganz today? Tell me you didn't."

"He wanted changes I couldn't live with."

"You told him he was full of shit."

"I said no such thing."

"It's what he heard."

"I'm sure the Ear Institute has got an opening."

"Paul Ganz is one of the best writers in town."

"And worst execs, Jer. They'll get wise to him before the year's out."

"Jesus, Alan when are you going to stop trying to prove yourself? You did that already. You're not riding your father's coattails anymore..."

"Where to from here?"

"NBC's still trying to cast a writer for the Hutton bio. Let me see what I can do."

"Luck."

"Call you."

He hung up as the front doorbell rang. Crossing to it, he opened the door and stared. Standing there in the late-day sun was the woman he had seen at the rear of the chapel.

"Mr. Fitzgerald?"

"Yes?"

"My name is Maka Mahpiya," she said. "I'm a U.S. Marshall working on a case with the Lakota Pine Ridge Reservation in South Dakota. I wonder if you could spare a few minutes."

Yámni

3

In Alan's downstairs office Maka waited, pitched forward on the edge of a couch, smelling the coffee brewing from the kitchen above. She looked about. One wall, she saw, was a floor-to-ceiling bookshelf overflowing. Some, she realized, Milton and Chaucer, had to go back to college days. Another wall was filled with photographs and awards, an Emmy nomination, and two Writers Guild nominations. On one shelf was a Christopher Award. There was a computer, a printer, and phone. There was also a desk made of a wooden door, half of it resting on a waist-high file cabinet, the other end supported by pipes. Try as she might, she could never control her instinct for detail. For most of her career, she had been a careful investigator and a keen observer. She had been praised for her outstanding work and then recruited by the U.S. Marshals, her dream job from the beginning of her law enforcement career.

Footsteps on the stairway preceded Alan's entrance, tray in hand, with two mugs of steaming coffee, a bowl of sugar, and a carton of cream. The late-day sun, slanting in through the window that overlooked the canyon below, was striking her face. He saw her two large almond-shaped eyes, and full lips. He strained to find the right metaphor. The idea that such a sensual image could generate sexual thoughts came crashing down as

"

he saw the wedding ring on her finger. Setting the tray on a side table, he handed her a mug.

"Black's fine," she said, ignoring sugar and cream. She carried her mug back over to the bookcase and pulled a picture frame off the shelf. It was clearly a family photo taken at the studio, father, mother, siblings, and a young Alan. She tilted it toward Alan so as to ask a question without words.

"My family," Alan answered.

"You were in the movie business at a young age?" she stated but asked at the same time.

Alan hesitated, but answered, "My father was a producer and writer for the studio."

Maka put the frame back where she had found it and walked back towards Alan to sit with him.

"Little nepotism?" Maka said with a smile.

Alan didn't see much humor in the statement. "No, you have to earn your career in this business. Some ways, having a successful parent can make it more challenging for someone to…" He stopped himself and quickly went back to Paythan. "I can't tell you anything more than what you heard me say at the service," he said, doctoring his coffee. "He had that alcohol problem, and then what they said."

"Who said?" She asked.

"The Mexican police in Tijuana. Hit by a motorcycle."

"They lied."

"I beg your pardon?"

"He wasn't hit by a motorcycle. I saw the body. He was beaten to death."

Whatever Alan had expected to hear, that wasn't it. He slumped into the chair across from the couch, words failing him for the moment, until: "*Beaten* to death."

"He was wearing an identification bracelet. They released his body to Lakota authorities who were suspicious of the findings. My office was called in. An autopsy was ordered. The result was as suspected. He'd been brutally beaten. Further, toxicology revealed he had an alcohol content way over permissible limit."

Alan hadn't touched his coffee, and he didn't now. He was sick to his stomach.

"What'd the Mexican authorities have to say?" he asked.

"The Mexicans wanted nothing to do with it," she answered. "Neither did the Americans."

"Jesus."

"If only."

"And you're out to find out what happened."

She nodded her head yes. He shook his.

"I don't know what else I can tell you."

She reached inside her oversized purse and took out a small card. He wondered if she had a weapon inside it.

"What was your relationship with him?" She asked.

"Pretty much the same as most of the students." *But damn, that wedding ring!* "We'd meet three hours once a week on Thursdays in class at the school. Several of them would come here on occasion for a couple of hours. We'd work on their projects."

"Paythan?"

"I asked him where his name came from, Burke. It wasn't Indian. Settlers, he told me. Indians often took their names."

"What would he talk about?"

"Well, he seemed fixated with something he called Waktoglasa."

"Waktoglaka," she corrected him. "It means to tell of one's victories."

"He was obsessed with Crazy Horse, who led the Lakota and Cheyenne against Custer."

"Is that what he was writing about?"

"If he was, he hadn't gotten to it in what he'd written. But he was fascinated by Crazy Horse. In some ways, disappointed."

"Really."

"That's what I gathered. We never really talked much about it."

She sat back, thinking that over.

"I'd like to read what he's written," she said. It wasn't a request.

"Of course."

He went to the file cabinet that supported his desk and opened the bottom drawer. Everything, she saw, was neatly filed. He pulled out a document, held together by round-head fasteners, and handed it to her.

"I'll be talking to his fraternity," she said, accepting the pages.

"They seemed just as bewildered by his disappearance as I was," he told her.

She nodded, accepting the likelihood, started to hand him the card she was holding, then pulled it back.

"I'm staying at the Ramada Plaza West." She produced a pen and jotted down a phone number on the back of the card. "This is my cell and the hotel's address and phone. If anything comes to mind, please call me."

She rose to leave. He followed her up the stairs to the front door, opened it, and turned to her.

"I'm sorry," he said. "I wish I could be more helpful."

She studied him a moment with a look he couldn't decipher.

"We'll see," she said, and was gone.

Exhausted, he ordered a brisket sandwich and beer delivered from Greenblatt's down on Sunset, half-finished it, and threw himself into bed at nine. The coyotes in the canyon were howling in unison like a chorus of unruly children. He tried to erase the day. He couldn't.

The phone awoke him at eight forty-five.

"Be in Stan Barrett's office at two-thirty."

Stan Barrett was a program executive of NBC's television movie division.

"Who's this?"

"Loberg. Jerry. Your agent," came the answer, in an irritated tone.

It didn't sound like Jerry. The voice was thick and unrecognizable. When Alan saw him in the NBC lobby, he realized why. He looked like he'd taken a high inside fastball and hadn't ducked. He'd been jogging with his dog that morning, Stan explained. On a leash, it suddenly cut in front of him, going for a squirrel, and tripped Jerry, who fell to the pavement, knocking out two teeth. Still, he was grinning, which was usual.

Stan Barrett's office was unpretentious. He rose to greet Alan and Jerry as they entered, a large, grey-suited well-kept African American, the first Black entertainment executive Alan had encountered. With pleasantries concluded, coffee delivered, Barrett webbed his fingers together, looked at Alan. Barrett had the feeling Alan wasn't the right writer for this project.

"Ever see *The Miracle of Morgan's Creek?*" he asked.

Alan assured him that he had.

"What'd you think?"

"The Hays Office, motion picture censorship in its day , must have been asleep when the picture was released."

"I meant Betty Hutton. What do you know about her?"

"At this point? Not much. Big star in the forties. Fell on hard times. Died a decade ago…"

"We want to do a Movie of The Week, a MOW, on her life," Barrett interrupted.

Alan nodded, understanding Barrett's hesitation. Hutton was a woman. Alan wasn't.

"He can do this. He's your guy," Jerry jumped in. "Research is his game. Also, he has the ability to put himself into the character he's portraying." He rattled off what Alan had done, capturing unfamiliar people and worlds.

The look on Barrett's face registered his ambivalence. The days of the TV movie, the so-called MOW, once a major staple of network programming in the seventies and eighties, was now a thing of the past. Cost and television viewership concentration, thought to be at best no more than an hour, had shrunk MOW orders. Still, the occasional special made the network schedule and Alan was one of the writers trusted to pull it off. With that, there was no one more vulnerable than a studio or network executive waiting for a writer to turn in his pages. Was he really going to pull it off? Or was he going to put the executive out of business?

"When can I hear a pitch?" Barrett asked.

Alan hated that word. Industry slang had a cheapness to it. But by agreeing to ask for it, NBC would have to commit to a full-on no-cut contract, outline, and first draft. Then rewrite and polish. Alan had reached a status where he could command it. It was a calamitous investment if he turned out a turkey.

"When do you need it?" he asked.

"Yesterday," Barrett answered.

The north campus research library at UCLA was Alan's special haunt. Most writers he knew relied on Google for their research, which he found superficial. The campus library's shelves on virtually any given subject were voluminous and his target.

Heading to the university from NBC, he found the north campus parking lots filled. He made his way to one with an opening half a mile away and just south of the John Wooden Center, gathered a newly purchased journal from the seat beside him, and locked his car. He crossed to the Janz steps, climbed them to the main campus complex, went past Royce Hall, came finally, breathless, to his destination and entered.

There were three books, in particular, he had intended to start with in researching the late Betty Hutton: *Backstage You Can Have My Own Story, Rocking Horse, A Personal Biography,* and *Betty Hutton Scrap Book.* But something else invaded his preoccupation. He acceded to it, searched for it on the ground floor location computer, climbed the stairway to the designated floor, and found what he'd been searching for: Lakota Indian sociology, people, history, and lore. Selecting two books, he crossed to an empty desk chair, sat down, and had opened the first, *The Lakota Way,* when his cell phone rang. Eluding annoyed looks from students who were trying to concentrate on their own subjects, Alan rose, sought sanctuary in an alcove, and answered the call. It was not, as he had expected, his agent.

"Mr. Fitzgerald?" a woman's voice asked.

"Yes?"

"Maka Mahpiya. I need to talk to you again. Can we meet somewhere?"

A slight tremor went through him. He couldn't help it. There was simply something about this woman.

"Miss Mahpiya, I told you all that I know," was all he could think to say.

"Tonight, if you can," she answered, ignoring his response.

He thought for a minute. There was an urgency in her voice.

"Dinner okay?" he asked.

She seemed to think that over before agreeing.

"There's a restaurant near you, Lucque's. One of the best in town," he said. "Seven okay?"

"I'm on a limited budget."

"It's on me. I'll make a reservation, pick you up at a quarter to."

"I'll meet you there," she said with what he sensed was arm's-length caution and no little indifference.

"Seven," he repeated, concealing annoyance. "The hotel will give you the address."

"Seven o'clock," she confirmed and hung up, leaving him holding a dead phone. Whatever thoughts he had about this woman, married or not, she bloody well made it clear. Forget about it.

Lucque's was located on Melrose, just east of La Cienega, already nationally famous before President Barack Obama had dinner there. Arriving at ten minutes to seven, Alan entered to find Maka already seated.

"Any trouble finding the place?" he asked. Stupid question. She was there, wasn't she?

"No trouble," she said.

He slid onto a chair opposite her and looked her over. She'd changed into a simple pants suit. On the cloth-covered bench seat beside her were Paythan's forty pages, half dozen yellow post-its protruding from them. She already had a menu before her and had looked it over with some astonishment.

"These prices," she said.

"The whole town's overpriced," he answered.

"Thirty-four dollars for *duck?* My father and I used to go hunting for them. It cost the price of a shotgun shell."

"Life on the reservation?"

"So long as duck was all you were after."

They were interrupted by the arrival of their waiter.

"Evening, Mr. Fitzgerald."

"Francis." Alan turned to Maka. "Wine?"

"Sprite," she said.

"J and B and soda for me," Alan said. He looked to Maka again. "You've looked over the menu."

"Whatever," she said, seemingly overwhelmed by the choices.

"We'll both do the duck," Alan said, turning back to the waiter.

"Good choice," Francis nodded, which is what was always said regardless of the order as he retreated.

"They know you here," Maka said.

"They know *everyone* here," he answered, "until you get two bad reviews."

She wasn't sure she understood. She smiled anyway.

"You were raised on the reservation?" he asked.

"Born and bred."

"How'd you get into police work?"

"When I graduated from high school the Council came to me. They'd send me through college - South Dakota State - if I'd guarantee them four years after I got out."

"That must have been pretty flattering.

"At the time, not really. They wanted men. Problem was the guys would get to the university, cut their hair short, change their name to Zarabosky, and take off for Kansas City or Memphis."

"But you're still with it."

"After my four years was up, I joined the FBI, spent a short stint with ICE, and was recruited by the U.S. Marshals. Thirteen years now."

"What's your husband do?"

"What husband?"

"You're wearing a wedding ring."

"Not married. Never have been. The ring's for defense."

A rush, like warm water, ran through him.

"Your turn," she said.

He anxiously wanted to stay on the subject just opened, wisely thought better of it, and addressed her question.

"I was born in San Francisco. Mother an RN, Dad was a writer/producer. I tried to get into Berkeley. Nobody gets into Berkeley unless you're a four-star quarterback. I ended up at San Jose State, as an English major, took a writing course. The professor and I did not get along. I challenged his approach to teaching writing, he challenged my ability. 'You'll never be a writer,' he told me. 'If you do write, it won't sell. If it sells, it won't be read. If it's read, it won't be remembered." He paused. "I give him credit for one thing, though."

Her eyebrows raised in question.

"He was one hell of a motivating force." A pause. "Want more?"

She gestured; his choice.

"Married soon after college - good girl, she truly was - but we were never really in love. Her parents liked me, my parents liked her, which was the reason for tying it on. She hated the business. I'd come home with a job, she'd say 'What about the next one?' She'd have been happier if I'd been a fry cook at Denny's as long as it was steady. We divorced after two years. No children. She ended up marrying a doctor and having three kids."

They'd completed the preliminaries. The awkward silence between them established it. She picked up Paythan's forty pages and placed them before her on the table as their drinks arrived.

"You've read this," she said.

"Of course."

"I mean *read* it, understood what he was writing about?"

"Okay, I'm not a hundred percent sure about that," he said, leveling. "What am I missing?"

"To begin with," she said, "how'd he end up in Tijuana?"

"He went there after school was out."

"He went home to Pine Ridge. That's South Dakota, not Mexico." Alan seemed surprised.

"I didn't know that. How *did* he end up in Tijuana?"

"That's the job."

"Where do you begin?"

She picked up her Sprite, took a sip, looked him over. "Besides his mother, you're the one person I know that spent time with him."

"His fraternity brothers?"

"Football and girls."

"I've told you everything I remember."

"If there's one thing I've learned over the years, it's that memories are a peculiar thing. You never know what can jar recall."

He studied her for a moment, knowing the question she was about to ask. "What are you asking?"

"Come back to Pine Ridge with me," she said.

His grip on his scotch and soda was so intense he thought the glass could break. "Look," he said, "I'm a writer, not a sleuth."

"Some people think that's one and the same."

"What people?"

"There are one-stop flights from Los Angeles to Rapid City. I'm flying out at eight in the morning. My car's at the airport there."

"Listen. I'm a professional writer. I write for a living. I'm on assignment."

She waited for him to go on. He did.

"I'm impacted by this, I really am. I hope to God you come up with the answer, but I could no more bail on my people than you could on yours." He waited for her to acknowledge his dilemma. She turned instead to the screenplay, opened it to the first post-it.

"You said he spoke to you about Crazy Horse. There were three with that name."

"I didn't know that."

"Few do. Whichever one he was talking about," she went on, "if that's what he was doing, Crazy Horse doesn't enter the script in these first forty pages."

"I think we better stop right there," he said.

"What he *has* written," she continued, "seems familiar, like he's dramatizing the foundation of a legend."

"Maka!" She stopped. "What are you doing?" he asked.

She looked at him.

"A boy," she said, "a Lakota Indian boy. Murdered. Brutally. Where was the television, the press? Not a mention. If it had been one of his white fraternity brothers, every paper in the country would have had it on the front page. Just a little savage loafer: the Lakota's life, legacy, insolence, drunkards with silly names like Bear Pipe, Two Cows, Stands On Ground, Stiff Leg, Black Kettle. What was he doing in Tijuana? Lakota do not go to the south! Go to the south, you die! What drew him there? Accident, stupidity, rage? What *was* it?"

Caught by the emotion behind her speech, Alan opened his mouth to reply when a stir went through the room. Turning, he saw what it was. Collin Royce, once a familiar motion picture leading man, now relegated to the little screen, was entering with a mini entourage. The problem was that he had come from the set where he was filming a western pilot, still dressed in costume. Black boots, black pants, black shirt, black hat, Marshal's badge pinned to his chest. It was a bizarre enough sight 'til ten feet into the room he was greeted by an up-and-coming comic doing his best Robin Williams imitation.

"Hey, big movie star! Doin' TV!"

The room broke into laughter. Suppressing his own, Alan turned back to Maka. She was gone.

The coyotes were doing their thing in the canyon below when Alan reached home. It was 8:45 and the message light on his phone was blinking.

"Alan? Jer." It was his agent. "Deal's set with the Hutton project. They wanted two showings before paying out rerun payments, and they wanted to split your fee, half to a producing credit to avoid paying full Writers Guild Health and Pension and they wanted a guarantee of script delivery in four weeks. Told them get another writer, they backed off. Start typing."

Alan glanced at his watch. Ten minutes to Rachel Maddow on MSNBC. He decided to pass - he would catch Lawrence O'Donnell at ten - went down to his office, picked up the first of the three Hutton bios he had checked out at the UCLA North Campus Library, and started in. Fifteen minutes later, he was staring at page twenty and hadn't the vaguest memory of what he'd been reading.

All that occupied his mind — and which blocked all else - was Paythan. Try as he could, he couldn't divorce himself from it. *Damn! Stop thinking about it! Not your problem, not your business!* He had known the kid, what, four months? *Get rid of it!* But was it his problem? "Where are you in your work?" It was his mantra and he had drilled it into his students. Was there something in those forty pages that should have alerted him, some clue to Paythan's psyche, his state of mind, that led to his death, and that Alan had missed?

He looked for the manuscript, and suddenly remembered he didn't have it. *She* did. He slumped back in his chair, elbows on armrests, hands cupping his cheeks. He sat that way for three minutes, then pulled forward. The hotel card she had given him was on his desk. He picked it up and reached for the phone. On the back of the card, she had written her cell number. He dialed it. After three rings, she came on the line.

"Maka? Alan," he said. "Get me ticketed on your flight tomorrow."

"Already did," she said.

Tópa

4

LAX to Salt Lake City, early lunch at the airport cafeteria there, transfer to Trans State Air to Rapid City, South Dakota, anticipated ETA 11:29 am. Except it wasn't going to happen. A fog over southern Nebraska was so thick that Alan, seated by the window, couldn't see the wing tip running light. The sound of the engines throttling back indicated a cautionary lowering of airspeed.

He had been through it before, two years ago, when flying into New York, seated first class thanks to the Writers Guild Management contract for writers on assignment. In a fog equally dense, flaps down, there was the grinding sound of the wheels lowering as the plane came in for its landing. Alan saw a head, two rows in front of his, emerge, turning as it took in the cabin. It was, Alan recognized, a 6'10" member of the Los Angeles Lakers.

"You know what he's looking for," Alan's seat companion growled. "Who gets top billing if this plane goes down."

On the Rapid City flight, Alan turned from the window, dropped the back of his head against the headrest, and glanced at Maka next to him. She had Paythan's classroom screenplay open and was reading it for perhaps the fourth time. He turned from her, closed his eyes, and took in a deep breath, drinking in her scent. He tried to identify it. Nothing artificial. No perfume. Yet it was sensual. Earthen. He tried to find another word. He couldn't. Earthen.

"Are you finding anything helpful in his manuscript?"

Maka flipped through the pages, "Not yet."

"May I?" Alan reached for the screenplay; she willingly gave it to him. He glanced through, skimming over the pages. He noticed a quote: "Chief Sitting Bull – before he was assassinated said, 'Upon suffering beyond suffering: *the Red Nation shall rise again, and it shall be a blessing for a sick world.* A world filled with broken promises, selfishness, and separations. A world longing for light again. I see a time of Seven Generations when all the colors of mankind will gather under the Sacred Tree of Life and the whole Earth will become one circle again.

And that day there will be those among the Lakota who will carry knowledge and understanding of unity among all living things. And the young white ones will come to those of my people and ask for this wisdom. I salute the light within your eyes where the whole universe dwells, for when you are at that center within you and I am in that place within me, we shall be as one."

Alan read it aloud. "That was beautifully said."

"Yes, in the Black Hills there are shadows of history lingering on the land and a new generation is continuing to fight. Looks like Paythan might have been a part of that fight. The loss of the Black Hills represents all the injustices the Lakota people have suffered. It's not just about the land, it is about the undoing what was done to the people."

Alan was speechless. He continued to read.

Breaking through the cloud cover, the plane touched down at the Rapid City Regional Airport without incident. Alan found, to his surprise, that the terminal was an isolated structure on the prairie, remarkably modern. Advertisements throughout its interior explained why. It was the gateway to Mt. Rushmore.

Retrieving their bags, Alan followed Maka from the terminal and was crossing with her to the parking area when a pick-up pulled up beside them. Two men were in it, both bald, mid-twenties, heavily adorned with swarms of tattoos. A Blackhawk Axiom multi-round rifle stretched across the rear window.

"S'matter, man," the passenger said, shoving his head out the window. "Can't find a white woman?"

Stunned, Alan dropped his suitcase to the concrete path and stared after the retreating pick-up.

"What'd he say?" he asked, and then repeated, *"What'd he say?"*

Responding as though she'd heard nothing at all, Maka nodded to the side. "My car's the next row."

A week of prairie dust and intermittent raindrops had painted the nine-year-old Jeep Wrangler a polka-dot grey. Wiping the windshield clean with a rag and squirts of bottled water, Maka followed Alan into the car. Leaving the airport, she rolled through the exit stop sign and turned south on an all but deserted highway marked SD 40. As the car began to accelerate, Alan flattened his back against his seat and glanced at the speedometer. It was eighty and climbing.

"How long to the reservation?" he asked.

"Depends," she answered.

"On what?"

"If the Highway Patrol's out."

Seeing it locked in at eighty-five, Alan looked about as the jeep plunged along through barren, rolling mixed-grass prairie land, the overhead cloud cover burning off. Windblown sands, he saw, formed dunes. Here and there were a scattering of scrub pines and cedar trees. A sign flashed by: "Pine Ridge Reservation – 93 miles."

"I thought it would be different," he said.

She glanced at him, eyes asking the question.

"Pine Ridge," he answered. "I thought it would be woods."

"This once was a sea," she said.

"What happened?"

"You're looking at it."

An hour and fifteen minutes later, a road sign that had been turned into a sieve by bullet holes, informed them: "Entering Pine Ridge Reservation."

Few things made Alan sick to his stomach. He'd seen poverty before, once, on a trip to Egypt. This matched it, as the road went from asphalt to dirt. Two miles in, they were attacked by an acrid odor as an immense dump came into view. Pungent smoke climbed from it. A pack of wild dogs scavenged for what they could find while crows circled with screeching impatience, awaiting their turn. A crudely written, misspelled sign protruded from its center, labeling the dump: "Genural Stor."

The further they went into the reservation, the more Alan saw it. Broken down plywood houses "For Rent." An equally broken-down bus, abandoned pickups, decaying and half-dismembered for parts. Rusted-out trailers flanked teepees, participants emerging from one, steam pouring out from a purification ceremony. They drove past a graveyard filled to overflowing with wooden crosses and plastic flowers; past a bare-chested brave trudging along the road, deep scars on his chest from the once-sacred Sun Dance ceremony; past a child outside her trailer home, being washed by her mother in a metal tub among the family's dishes. A weathered church boarded up. Kids standing atop a junk pile, others climbing over fences, staring at the passing jeep. Suddenly, four young natives, aged fourteen and fifteen, bareback on horses, crude war clubs in hand, galloped alongside Maka for fifty yards, then disappeared over a hill. They passed a sign reading: "Alcohol Is Not Allowed on Reservation." Half was scratched out, replaced by: "Legalize Alcohol!"

Alan sat back, eyes forward, jaw tight, one thought burning through his brain: *How the hell did I get into this?*

Forty minutes later, they reached the unincorporated town of Rosebud, euphemistically designated a town, on the banks of Rosebud Creek. There was a fuel plaza featuring truck parking, a convenience store, a coffee shop, and bodega market, along with a motel and mini-casino. Turning off the main onto a side road, Maka pulled to a stop before a cramped modular building. A sign designated it as: "Wazi Ahanhan Akicita Okolakiciye." The translation below it was: "Pine Ridge Police Department." A couple of squad cars stood in the street. To one side was a large trailer, marked "Police," which served as administration offices.

Across the street, Alan noticed a lumber yard. Something was going on. A dozen Lakota in work clothes were gathered, roughly six on a side, listening to the exhortations of a lone man in the middle. Occasionally one or two would switch sides.

"What's going on?" Alan nodded toward the event.

"It's a trial," Maka explained.

"For what?"

"One of the men seduced another man's wife. They're determining punishment, something he has to give up of equal value."

"Like what?"

"As an example? His bicycle."

In an overstaffed twelve by twenty room that he shared with half a dozen staffers, Jeremy Hurd, Chief of Police for the Pine Ridge Reservation, rose to greet Alan as Maka led him in. At fifty-eight, six-four, two hundred fifty pounds of well-earned muscle, Hurd, Lakota born, possessed gnarled hands, an ancient slash wound across one cheek, and an infectious welcoming grin.

"Chief, Alan Fitzgerald," Maka led off the introductions. "Alan, Chief Hurd."

"Welcome to the land of Custer's final!" Hurd said in a booming voice as he thrust out a gigantic paw.

"What was he thinking?" Alan beamed, accepting Hurd's paw.

"He was thinking he needed a calling card for the 1876 Democratic presidential nomination," Hurd answered, then switched subject, "Let's get out of here."

The Higher Ground Coffee Shop, three forty-five by the clock above the counter, was otherwise deserted as Hurd heaved himself into one of two booths already occupied by Maka and Alan. There were three cups of coffee in his hands. He deposited one before each of them.

"Maka tells me you're a writer," he said to Alan.

"I am."

"TV," she said.

"Rosanne?"

"Never have."

"Don't know how her husband puts up with her."

"You're not the first to ask."

"How do you get into that business?"

"By not being qualified for anything else."

Hurd's roar of approval shook the room. "Write mysteries?"

"Who doesn't?"

"Always thought my life would make a good story. Just needs someone to put down the words…You're laughing."

"I'd like a dime every time I've heard that."

Hurd's expression indicated that he shared the humor of Alan's retort. He took a sip of his coffee and set the mug on the table. His countenance changed. "How much do you know about Paythan?"

"As I told you on the phone, Chief -" Maka started to reply.

"Let me hear from him," Hurd cut her off.

"I had him in class." Alan thought back to his time with the youth. "We spent time together. At school and my house."

"And?"

"He was a different student than the others I had then. Most liked to write about things they knew nothing about. War, for example, and sex. Paythan had something he wanted to say."

"Like what?"

"Curiously, we never got that far, at least not far enough for me to give you a specific analysis. He didn't like to talk about where he was going. But Crazy Horse was his major fixation."

"Little Big Horn?"

"Little Big Horn, I sensed, was only part of it. A steppingstone to something else he had in mind."

"Such as?"

"He never told me. He did tell me Crazy Horse was a simple, modest man, beloved by the Lakota as a brilliant, courageous tactician in battle. But I sensed that as much as he admired Crazy Horse, he was at the same time disappointed in him."

"He never told you why?"

"He said he was working it out. It'd turn up in the writing."

Hurd sat back slowly, going over in his mind what he had to say.

"We've got a murder," Hurd said at length, "and damn few clues. We know he came back to Pine Ridge when school let out. We know one month later, his body was found in Tijuana. That makes no sense. If he was going to go to Mexico to blow off steam after finals, he'd have gone directly there. He didn't. He came home and went to work at *The Pine*

Ridge Free Press writing obituaries, a full-time job around here. So, what do you bring to the table, Kola?"

"Kola?" Alan queried, not understanding the word.

"Male friend," Maka explained.

"I'm as much in the dark as you are," Alan said.

"Then why are you here?"

"He spent more time with Paythan than anyone we know right before his death," Maka said. "I'm betting on recall he hasn't come up with yet."

Alan drew in a deep breath and released it slowly.

"Damn, I don't know," He thought a moment, then, "Have you talked to the newspaper people where he worked?"

"It was the first thing we did," Maka said.

"What'd you get from them?"

"Good worker, quiet, kept to himself."

"Who runs the thing?" Alan asked.

"Adam Red Fox," Hurd answered.

"Lakotan?"

"Oglala Sioux."

Hurd got a call, looked at his phone, stood to leave. "Keep me posted if you recall anything. I want to get to the bottom of this, after all, the reservation did invest in his education."

Záptaŋ

5

The Pine Ridge Free Press was one of two papers on the reservation, the *Free Press* the far lesser of the two. Located in a converted barn, with a staff of three since Paythan's departure, it was a weekly, dedicated to the memory of far better days. Written and assembled in a four-page mock-up, it was delivered to a print shop in Rapid City each Friday and picked up the following Monday for distribution. The paper was published in English, native tongue, with rare exception, lost to the past.

The owner, managing editor, Adam Red Fox, had earned a bronze star for bravery in Iraq and an education from South Dakota University, majoring in English Lit, of all things. He was a slight man, dressed in jeans, lumberman's shirt, horned rimmed glasses, and golf cap. Unlike many of his generation, he had never Americanized his name but stuck to the tribal original.

Pulling a file from a makeshift cabinet behind his desk, Adam Red Fox removed a grouping of rolled-up papers bound by a rubber band, turned to Alan and Maka seated across from him.

"He was here a month," Adam Red Fox said, "writing obituaries. Twenty-two of them, which seemed more than usual at the time, but here they are." He laid the bound pages on his desk before them. "No question he was a writer. He had a style, even with obits."

"Style?" Alan asked.

"Read one."

Alan removed the rubber band and flattened the pages. Maka reached across, took the top one, Alan the next, both perusing the separate texts.

"Raymond Blue Dun died on June 7th at the age of 52," Alan began to read aloud. "Affectionately known as Three Finger Blue due to a confrontation with a circular saw twelve years ago, he enjoyed hunting, proudly displaying the stuffed skunk he shot back in 1996 trophy-style on his wall, much to the dismay of his wife, Little Whispering Elm, who survives him. His fondness for Spaghetti Westerns was only surpassed by his love of buffalo bacon, beer, and sunkawakan."

Alan looked at the publisher. "Sunkawakan?"

"Horse," Maka translated.

Alan nodded, appreciating the wit.

"When was the last time you saw him?" Maka asked.

"He left after work one night. It was a Wednesday. Mid-week, mid-June. Never returned. We asked around. Nobody'd seen him. Even called his school in L.A. Nothing. 'Til we heard about Tijuana."

"Where did he live here?" Maka asked.

"With a woman named Elinor Fields."

"His mother?" she questioned, writing down the name.

"His parents passed when he was in middle school. They split all the kids up, Elinor only adopted him."

"Lakotan?" Alan asked.

"Caucasian. She's a teacher at the local high school."

"Where does she live?" Maka asked.

"A couple of miles from here."

"On the reservation?" Alan said, surprised by the answer.

"Has for twenty years. The school can tell you."

"Who took in the other kids?" Alan asked.

"The older two ran away, the younger girl was placed into foster care."

"Did he ever mention anything about going down to Mexico?" Maka asked.

"From what I know, it was the last thing on his mind. He was looking forward to his final year at the university…"

"There was his history with alcohol," Maka cut in.

"Yeah, we all knew he'd had a battle with that. But I didn't notice anything while he was with us."

"They found alcohol in his system when they did the autopsy," she said.

Adam Red Fox shook his head. "I'm not qualified to give an opinion on that one."

Maka turned to Alan. "Mr. Fitzgerald?"

"You're suggesting it could have warped his sense of reason?" Alan asked her.

"It's happened," she answered.

Alan thought a moment, shook his head, nothing further to offer.

Maka turned to the publisher. "May I take these?" she said, referring to the obituaries. "I'll have them Xeroxed and get them back to you."

"No problem," he said.

She rose, the two men rising with her.

"Thanks for your help," Alan said, offering his hand.

"Where do you think you're going with this?" Adam Red Fox asked.

"At the moment...?" Alan started to answer. He broke off and looked to Maka.

"We'll keep you posted," she said.

Šákpe

6

In Maka's car, Maka and Alan sat for a moment staring out at the fading twilight. It was not a pretty sight, grey-black clouds covering what was left of the day. Starting the engine, Maka threw her car into gear and pulled away from the Free Press office.

"I tried to get you in at the Prairie Wind Hotel, but it's closed for renovation, so it's the Oglala Lodge. It's got a restaurant," she said. "It's not that far."

"I've got a question," Alan said.

"Go."

"What just happened in there?"

"You mean what was Paythan doing in Mexico?"

"Not close."

"What're you talking about?"

"Mister Fitzgerald," he quoted her. *"Mister?"*

She thought for a moment, then, "It's a defensive respect you learn here early."

"You're kidding."

"When's the last time you saw whites respectful of us? You saw what happened at the airport."

She glanced at him and saw him thinking that over. "I'm waiting."

"Self-deprecation is an act that generally results in no positive outcome," he said.

"Is that what you think this was?"

"Isn't it?"

"You come from a place where acceptance is a primary word in your way of life, it's rarely challenged. There are a hundred different languages spoken where you come from. Here it's one."

"You make it sound like a hostile climate."

"Not so long as you're willing to say *Mister*." They drove on in silence for a few minutes more.

"This isn't the south in the fifties," he said at length.

"A lot more similarities than you think."

"You've got schools."

"Home to asbestos, mold, and rats. Students have to carry their seats from class to class, presumably because the schools can't afford chairs for each classroom."

He reflected on that one, then: "What are you doing here?" he asked at length, a slightly punishing tone in his voice. "You're smart, attractive, educated. You could make it anywhere you went. You've served your penance."

"That's what you call it?"

"What else?"

"There's a history here that was great."

"Once. Two hundred years ago," Alan answered. "Rome was great once, Greece was great, Egypt too. They never came back."

He waited for Maka to answer.

"You like history? Between the time Columbus arrived in 1492 and the beginning of the 21st Century the population of over 80 million Native Americans was reduced by 90%.

The children don't know where they came from, or who they are. We excel so much at being white, we forget our teachings from our culture of who we are. Without knowing who they are they are lost and get involved with drugs, alcohol, and toxic relationships. Kids on the res live with a hopeless feeling of constant assimilation, they don't want to learn. No motivation to learn what it is to be Lakota." She paused for a moment.

"Ten minutes," she added.

The Oglala Lodge and Casino, so identified by a sign above its entrance, sixty dollars a night with a Triple A card, was akin to a quirky, old one-story wooden motel attached to a small casino.

Pulling to a stop before the entrance, Maka stared out at the place with Alan. "Sorry," she started to apologize. "We can try someplace else…"

"No sweat," he said, catching the unhappy scent of greasy frying food. "Bite before you go?"

"I've got a night's work ahead of me. I'll see you here at nine-thirty,"

"Dining room?"

"See you then,' she said.

He nodded, stepped from the car, and opened the rear door for his luggage.

"Word of warning," she stopped him.

"Salmonella?"

"Stick to the burgers," she said, drew closed the passenger side door, threw her car into gear, and was gone.

The room Alan engaged was modest in size which was the best of it. Worn, outdated bed, tired ripped chairs, stained walls, and an ancient black and white TV. There was a wall safe, secured by personal code. Not having eaten since the Salt Lake City airport earlier that day, he left for the restaurant and ordered the burger plate which came barely warm and overcooked. Worse was the service, slow and disinterested. Topping it off with a cup of stale coffee, he paid his bill, wandered into the lobby.

There was a desk, on it a summoning bell, but no one on duty. There were a couple of plastic chairs, the sort that could be stacked, one on the other. There was a door to the street, another to the casino, and a large clipboard advertising tours of the reservation. There was also something else that caught Alan's attention, that he'd missed earlier when he'd arrived. On the walls were a dozen cheaply framed ancient photographs of Lakota and Sioux survivors of Little Big Horn.

Alan wandered to them, took them in one by one. Dressed in deer hides, hair ties wrapped around doubled-up braids, faces painted in bright war paint, some with animal designs, some with multi-feathered headdresses, they variously held in their hand spears, buffalo-hide shields, rifles. Below the photographs were their names: Standing Alone, Kills In The Water, White Cloud, and Charging Bear. All possessed threatening scowls.

Perusing one after the other, Alan suddenly stopped, captured by one in particular. A Lakota of average height, early thirties, he wore a single hawk's feather protruding from his hair. His braids, wrapped in fur, fell across his buckskin shirt. He wore no beads, no adornments, was devoid of war paint, stood hands clasped before him, possessed no weapon. But the eyes. A chill went through Alan as they bore into his. His Lakota name, inscribed below his photo in his native tongue, was Char-O-Ha. Above that, in English, it read Crazy Horse.

The following morning, promptly at nine-thirty, showered and shaved, Alan came from his room to find Maka already seated in the restaurant over a cup of coffee. Beside it, laid out on the table, were Paythan's obituaries.

"Morning," Alan said.

"Morning," she replied. "How'd you sleep?"

"Some things are better not asked," he said with a grin, sliding onto the chair across from her.

She nodded. "I've got a thought about that. Pack and check out…"

She broke off as a waitress arrived. An Oglala Indian, she wore a vintage button-down dress shirt, skirt, and apron.

"Breakfast?" Alan asked Maka.

"Did. At home."

"Coffee for me," he said to the waitress. "Nice and hot, no cream. And toast. Whole wheat if you have it. I'll butter it."

The woman scratched the order on a pad and withdrew.

"Did you try the casino?" Maka asked.

Alan shook his head, no. "I've got a loser's mentality," he said. "But I saw the photographs in the lobby."

"The Little Big Horn survivors. Crazy Horse?"

"Yes."

"Not what you expected."

"No."

"Paythan's fascination."

"From what I recall."

She turned to the obituaries.

"I was up 'til two last night with these, made some calls this morning," she said.

"How'd it come out?"

"Good, fine, except for one."

"What do you mean?"

She took one off the top, handed it to Alan.

"Read it."

Alan hesitated, not certain of the reason for her request, took the obituary and began to read aloud.

"William Bunch, nee Fearing The Hawk, died from a rattlesnake bite Thursday. He was nineteen years old. He will be laid to rest at Whispering Cedar Cemetery Saturday at seven PM, Section 7D. He asks to please make note of his new address."

"There," Maka interrupted.

Alan looked up. "There what?"

"Whispering Cedar Cemetery hasn't had an interment on those grounds for twenty years, Section 7D hasn't been occupied since 1893. Further, there's no one on this reservation named William Bunch."

"How do you know that?"

"Checked with the phone and utility companies this morning. Checked with the DMV. Ran a check of birth records. No William Bunch."

Alan stared at Maka. He didn't know what to say.

"What do you make of this?" he asked.

"What do you?"

Alan turned back to the text and continued his reading.

"…please make note of the address. His headstone reads, 'I'll be back.' He respectfully requests six Chicago Cubs pallbearers, so the Cubs can let him down one last time."

He clutched the eulogy utterly buffaloed by it.

"Jesus," is all he could come up with. Then added, "This ended up in the *Free Press?*"

"It did," Maka admitted.

"For anyone to read?"

She nodded, yes.

"But of no interest to anyone who didn't know a William Bunch," he said.

She nodded again.

"So what was Paythan trying to do with this? What was he up to?"

"A thought does come to mind," she said.

"Some sort of message? A modern-day smoke signal?"

"That was the thought."

"To whom? For what?"

She sat back, shook her head, and had no idea as Alan's toast and coffee arrived. The toast, he noticed, was burnt and buttered.

"Where do we start?" he asked, pushing the toast aside when the waitress was gone.

"I'd like to see that cemetery," she said.

Taking State Route 83 north through the desolate heart of the reservation, they drove in silence. The road narrowing to barely two lanes, it came, at length, to an unmarked rutted dirt road off the main running west. Maka slowed the car to a stop. Activating a dashboard computer, she verified their location, looked up the road, and saw it disappearing through a hillock a half mile away. She sat for a moment in contemplation.

"Been here before?" he asked.

"No."

Throwing the car into gear, she headed in on a bone-jarring two-mile ride that suddenly broke onto a four-acre depression designated by a barely readable weathered chipped wooden sign as Whispering Cedar Cemetery.

Braking to a stop, Maka and Alan stared out at the dozens of neglected headstones and crosses, some tipping eerily at angles, others uprooted from their foundations, lying grotesquely on the ground. Nowhere was there a tree, not even scrub brush, nor any sign of life, not man nor animal. It was, Alan thought, the saddest sight he'd ever seen.

"7D his eulogy read," Maka said.

"What's that mean?" Alan asked.

"Seven rows in, four up," she answered.

She opened her car door and got out.

"Watch for rattlesnakes," she said as he followed.

Seven rows in, four from the left, they came to an abandoned grave site with a turned-over stone marked *William Bunch, 1852-1871 RIP*.

Driven into the ground, directly above the grave, was a lance, a half dozen hawk feathers attached to its top, reaching out, Maka pulled it from the earth.

"What is that?" Alan asked.

Maka turned it over in her hands. It was a painted wooden pole, nearly six feet long, attached to a metal spear point.

"It's a lance," she said.

"A what?"

"A war lance."

He looked about, trying to process what she'd said, settled on:

"That's it. There's nothing else here."

"There is," she said, settling onto her haunches. On the ground was a scattering of a dozen freshly cut eight-to-ten-inch sticks, thrown down. She picked up one, turned it over in her fingers. Their ends, she saw, were cut at a precise angle, cleanly sliced through. Alan looked at her, eyes asking the question.

"There's an old Lakota warrior custom," she said. "Throw your sticks onto the pile, if you're ready for war."

The shock on Alan's face was palpable as Maka slowly rose, flicking dirt from her fingertips. Turning, she started back to her car. Nothing else to do, Alan followed, his soft leather Gucci loafers scarring and filling with dirt. He was sure he heard the familiar rattle of a rattlesnake. But Maka gave no notice of hearing anything. Reaching her car, he followed her inside, closed his door, and sat with her staring out at the cemetery. Starting the car, she continued to stare out at the grave sites.

"What was he doing?" she asked in genuine confusion. "There's nothing to fight for here, it's over, finished, done. All we have is this, the Bad Lands. What was he after?"

A moment more she lingered on the cemetery, dropped the car into gear, circled to the access road, took it back to the highway, and turned south toward Rosebud.

Shoulders bunched, eyes locked on the empty road ahead, Alan reflected on two things. One, he was out of his league. He actually knew, he realized, next to nothing of Paythan, certainly far less than Maka.

The second was far more daunting. All of his professional life he'd written about the adventures and exploits of others, dangerous, fulfilling, courageous, cowardly, tragic, and desperate--always from the outside, looking in. Now, for the first time, he was the centerpiece of his exploration. He was the one on the line, and which one of the above was he?

He glanced at Maka. Her jaw was set. What was going through her brain? Was she analyzing what she'd just discovered at the grave site? Or had she figured him out? He looked forward again and imperceptibly shook his head in self-disdain. If she hadn't come to recognize his ineptitude she would soon enough, that much he knew.

Then…wait a minute! His self-flagellation was not only misplaced, but it was also absurd. Since when did he see himself as a sleuth? Further, what had truly drawn him into this? His sense that somehow, he'd missed the signs in his conversations with Paythan? Nonsense! It was Maka. Never one to pass the lure of such an enticing woman, *that's* what had hauled him in, right? Right? So how to get out of it gracefully, get on the first plane out tomorrow back to L.A. Jerry, his agent, he'd call him. Let Jerry scream bloody murder at him for running off to South Dakota on some perceived adventure when he should be tackling his teleplay for NBC. That was it. Blame it on Jerry, who'd warn him the network wouldn't tolerate this nonsense. He'd tell Maka, *Sorry, I'm under dire threat of breaching my contract and facing industry expulsion if I don't get home and get to work.*

He sat back, eyes closed, his heart beating a tattoo in his chest.

Šakówin

7

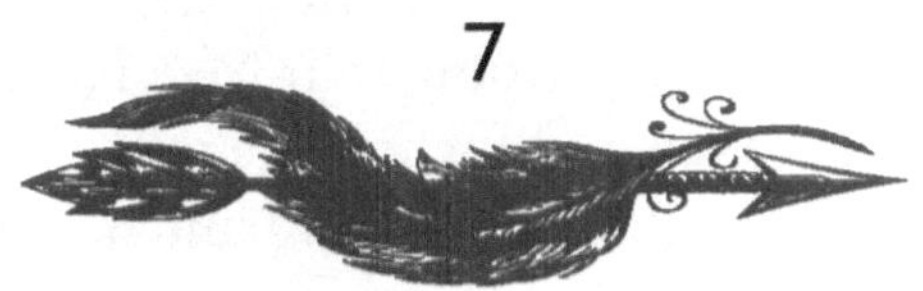

Returning to Rosebud, Maka slowed as she drove through the township. "What're we looking for?" Alan asked, the first words spoken since leaving the cemetery.

"Place for you to stay."

Coming to an off-road, she took it, a surprisingly well-maintained unpaved dirt lane, Alan noticed. Barrels of flowers, lavender pasques, members of the buttercup family, flanked it. A turn in the road brought them, not to the hotel or motel Alan expected, but to a one-story wood frame house. Unlike most of what he'd seen on the reservation, it was well kept, like the grounds around it.

Braking to a stop before the entrance, Maka cut the engine and opened her door.

"Bring your stuff," she said.

With no little bewilderment, Alan gathered his bag, followed her to the door, watched her unlock it, and disappear inside. The interior of the house, Alan found, as he entered, was the last thing he expected. An immaculate living room-dining area with a large oval oak table and chairs atop a traditional Lakota Indian rug occupied the center of the room off the kitchenette. Lakota artifacts adorned the place. Ancient bowls sat on a cabinet, a framed grouping of arrowheads hung from an open wall space, along with a shield with a buffalo head painted on it. Against another wall was a desk bearing a computer, phone, printer, and files, a Lakota doll perched atop it. Across from it, occupying a third wall, floor to ceiling, was a detailed map of the reservation, spilling into Wyoming and Nebraska, capped by the northern and eastern Black Hills. There was a faux fireplace with ceramic logs. A hallway, off the room, passing a bathroom to two bedrooms at the end, the cedar paneling varnished. A light was blinking on the phone. Going to it Maka activated the message. "Adam Red Fox here. Give me a call when you're in."

"You're last room on the right. I'll fix some lunch," she said, picking up the phone, and dialing the number from memory.

It wasn't her directions that caught his attention. It was the map. Maka hung up on a busy signal.

"Last on the right," she repeated, turning to the kitchenette. "Lunch," she said.

Crossing to the map, Alan stared at it, held by something that was capturing recall.

"Ham on rye?" she asked.

"What?" he answered, distracted by what he was seeing.

"Ham okay?"

"Great."

He turned from the map with his suitcase, moved into the hall, pausing at the bathroom, and entered it. There was a shower stall, he saw, a toilet, sink, medicine cabinet above it, and a towel rack with freshly hanging towels. Relieving himself, he flushed, turned to the sink, washed his hands, hesitated as he caught himself in the mirror, stared at his image, trying to look into himself, a look of realization on his face. Drying his hands, he gave up on the bathroom and left with his bag.

The room he found to be small but tidy and clean. There was a twin bed, chest, chair, closet, and window. Lowering his suitcase to the bed, he joined it, and sat staring into space, his mind tumbling with what he'd discovered. Or thought he'd discovered. No, knew he'd discovered.

Rising, he left the room, returned to the living room-dining area, and took a chair at the table that gave him a clear view of the map.

"Mayonnaise, lettuce, okay?" came her voice from the kitchenette.

"Sure."

"Sprite or Coke?"

"Either one," he answered, still held by the map.

Four minutes later she returned with two sandwiches on paper plates along with two bottles of Coke, produced two paper napkins, and joined Alan at the table.

"I don't get it," she said shaking her head, "I just don't, I really don't. There isn't a thing on this reservation to go to war over."

"How long have you had this place?" he asked looking away from the map.

"Three years," she said. "It was a fixer-upper."

"Who did the work?"

"I did. Dad wanted a boy. The first gift I got when I turned thirteen was a saw and a hammer."

"What *about* your parents?"

"Gone. My mother four years ago, Dad year after that."

"You were close to your father."

"Very."

She saw him force a smile.

"You weren't with yours?"

Jesus, she was perceptive. "I loved him. Not sure I liked him."

"That must have been painful."

"Yeah, well. I wasn't the easiest kid."

She watched him turn back to the map.

"What's going on?" she said.

"Tell me about the Lakota," he said.

"What don't you know?"

"Assume nothing."

"The short version, okay. We're a tribe of Native Americans who lived on the Great Plains. Collectively we made up a confederation of seven Sioux tribes, each functioning independently as a small self-governing nation almost. The greatest grounds we occupied were the Paha Sapa, Black Hills, north of here, rich with buffalo, elk, and streams full of fish. Around 1730 the Cheyenne introduced the Lakota to horses. After that, we centered our buffalo hunts on horseback. The buffalo were sacred. They supplied clothing, cover, weapons, and food. They were taken only as needed 'til white hunters came in and slaughtered all they could for sale in the east. Eventually, the Fort Laramie Treaty acknowledged Lakota sovereignty over the Black Hills 'til gold was discovered and the government rescinded the agreement, leading to a succession of massacres as the Lakota fought to retain what they'd been promised."

"Crazy Horse and Little Big Horn."

"And Sitting Bull."

"How'd it end?"

"Crazy Horse convinced his people to surrender, that they couldn't defeat the whites. He was promised sanctuary, brought his people into Fort Robinson, and was betrayed and killed. You've seen what we're left with."

Alan nodded and washed a bite of his sandwich down with his Coke.

"Something's going on with you," she said. "What is it?"

"He was talking in class one day."

"He?"

"Paythan. He was giving the history of the Lakota, much like you just did. He talked about how important the Black Hills were to his people, how disappointed he was in Crazy Horse, whom he revered, for giving in to the whites."

He looked at Maka. She was staring at him, her oval eyes wide, knowing where he was going with this.

"You think he was after the Black Hills," she said, incredulous.

"I think it's where you should start looking for what happened to him."

"He was a *kid*. He was *twenty!*"

"Alexander The Great was twenty when he took over Macedonia."

Maka rose slowly from her chair, eyes on the map.

"Why didn't I see that?"

"No guarantee," he gestured. "It's a possibility."

The phone rang. Going to it, Maka picked up the receiver.

"Maka Mahpiya," she said.

The voice on the other end of the line caught her attention. Dropping onto the chair at her desk, she picked up a pen and notepad.

"Where again?" she asked, listening for a good thirty seconds, scratching notes on the pad. Then, "Yes, I've got that, thank you." She hung up and held her hand on the phone as she contemplated what she'd just been told.

"That was Adam Red Fox," she said. "We have an appointment."

"An appointment?"

"His name is Blue Bear. I've heard of him. He calls himself a medicine man."

"I didn't know they still existed."

"If you're given to the old ways. He wants to see us."

"When?"

"Tonight. Nine o'clock?"

"Where?"

"You'll see."

The rutted dirt road cut through the prairie, the headlights of Maka's Wrangler pushing back the limited foliage. A jackrabbit, cutting in front of the car, momentarily froze in the lights, barely made it to safety. Braking to a stop, Maka stared with Alan. Seated on a rock at the side of the road was a lone figure. Dressed in a short gown, a hunting shirt, a beaded belt, homespun pantaloons, and moccasins, his shaved head showed a scalp-lock trailing down the back of his neck. His age was difficult to tell in the light, but clearly was north of fifty.

Alan sat with Maka for a moment, staring out. Leaving the motor running, headlights on, she left the car. Alan hesitated, then followed as Maka approached the man with a casual, non-threatening stride and smile, hands fully exposed. Watching intently, Alan saw Maka offer an opening in her native language.

"Hau." (Hello).

"Tanyan yahi." (Welcome), came the answer.

"Taku eniciyapi he?" (What's your name?)

"Emac iyapi." (Blue Bear).

"Blue Bear," she repeated in English, then, "Iya wyoaglaka he?" (Do you speak English?)

"Yes."

"Iche. Please," she said. "You asked to see me."

The man squinted at her through the Wrangler's headlights nearly blinding his eyes.

"You knew Paythan Burke," Maka said.

"Ohan," (Yes) the Indian answered.

"What can you tell us?"

Alan saw Blue Bear turn and look at him questioningly.

"This is my friend," Maka assured him. "He knew Paythan too."

"He came to me, I warned him," Blue Bear said.

"Warned him."

"Do not go to the other side, I told him."

"The other side is afterlife," she said, "The other side is death."

"He would not listen. So he went."

"To the Black Hills? What was he looking for?"

"The old ways." He paused. "It's not what he found."

"What did he find?" she asked.

"They'd come on trails in wagons made of steel, as big as large ships, a party of men of such size that from the knee down their height was as great as the height of an ordinary man though he might be of great stature himself. Their limbs were all in proportion to the deformed size of their bodies, and it was a monstrous thing to see, their heads with yellow hair reaching to their shoulders. Their eyes were as large as small plates, their hands like hooks, and their mouths ran red. The habits of these giants were revolting to the Lakota who wished Heaven would wipe them off the earth. Such was Paythan's quest."

"In the Black Hills," Maka said.

"Ai."

"Where in the Hills?"

"The gully."

"What gully? Where?"

"The gully," he repeated.

With that Blue Bear turned and disappeared into the night.

"Emac iyapi!" she called after him.

He was gone.

***

Enemies came among us from the south. They killed a man and took two young women. A war party went south on their trail, I went with them. We trailed them for half a moon, it seemed, into a country I had never seen, caught up with them as they rejoined their village. We saw where they had put the two young women and made a plan.

There were six of us. That night two of us would set a fire east of the village, and two of us would do the same to the west. While the men of the village were busy putting out the fires, two of us would sneak in and take back our young women. The plan worked except for one thing: I was captured.

By dawn, our war party had escaped back to the north with our two young women. My captors were very angry, they made me a slave. All my clothing was taken from me. I was led around naked. I was made to work and pulled drag poles like a dog until my hands and knees were bleeding. They threw dirt in my face. Women pulled up their dresses and laughed, showing me that I was no longer a man. They gave me no food, so I had to fight with the dogs for scraps. At night they bound me hand and foot and stretched me between two poles. There was no way to escape. One night, it was cold and rainy and I was naked and shivering. Even the dogs curled up out of the rain when suddenly there appeared a giant bird. With a beak as sharp as razors, it cut through my bindings, and lifted me up and away. I turned, and looked into its face, into the largest most wonderful eyes I'd ever seen. A young woman was staring down at me. It was Maka!

Šaglógaŋ

8

Alan bolted upright in bed, breaking out of his dream, for the moment having no idea where he was. Slowly it came back to him. He was in the bedroom provided by Maka, in her house. He glanced at his watch in the dark, the luminous dial revealed the time, two fifteen. He looked toward the closed door to his room. A blush of light shone at the base of the door.

Turning to the table lamp beside his bed, he turned it on, picked up the book he'd been reading he'd found in Maka's collection *The Lakota Way,* by Joseph Marshall III, and reread the section that had inspired his nightmare. He'd never heard of the author, but damn, he could spin a tale.

He sat for a moment more, dressed in light sweatpants, a T-shirt, and socks. Putting the book aside, he rose and walked to the door.

The living room-dining area Alan found, as he entered from the hall, was illuminated. Maka, barefoot and wearing cotton pajamas, was seated at the center table with her back to Alan. For a moment, he watched her pore over two large open books. Approaching from behind he laid a comforting hand on her shoulder. Two seconds later he was writhing on the floor, clutching his ribs, Maka hovering above him fist clenched and cocked.

"Oh, my God!" she said, staring in shock.

"S'okay."

"I didn't know it was you!"

"I'm fine," he lied.

"I thought you were asleep!"

"I was stupid."

"No, I mean it, I'm so sorry. But next time, please, make it a frontal approach.

He wondered for an instant if there was more to that invitation than seemed, decided to abandon the thought, tried to rise, but couldn't.

"Take my arm," she said.

He did. God, she was strong, and he felt something else, her breasts against his shoulder as she helped him into a chair at the table.

"Where'd you learn that?" he asked recovering his breath. "The Academy?"

"High school," she said, returning to her chair.

He gestured toward the books.

"What's that?"

"An atlas and a history of the Black Hills."

"Needle in a haystack?

"So far," she said

"The gully?"

She nodded, yes.

"Your man didn't say *a* gully, he said *the* gully. Which is what?"

"A long narrow valley with steep sides," she explained, "usually containing a river." She shook her head. "Nothing."

"It can't be nothing or he wouldn't have said it," Alan answered.

"You're right, of course, you're right. But what, what was he telling me?" She turned to him, saw him rubbing his side. "You, okay?"

"Just a couple of broken ribs," he joked.

She laughed, a short laugh. "I know how that feels," she said.

"You?"

"When I was a kid, fifteen, we had a bull named Dynamite. It was in this enclosure. I was cleaning out its droppings when it came for me. He'd never done that before, slammed me up against the fence."

"What'd you do?"

"Played dead. He got bored. I waited till he turned away and made it out."

"It must have hurt like hell."

"If that's what hell's like."

"I got into something like that when I was a kid."

"What happened?"

"High school. I was a senior. There was this guy, George. He had it in for me, had it in for a lot of guys, but I was it that day, goaded me into a fight. He was big-bigger than I was."

"What'd you do?"

"Wished I'd had someone like you with me. I didn't. You remember 'Butch Cassidy and the Sundance Kid'?

"Sure."

"Well, there's this scene just after the opening where Butch is challenged by this huge guy. Butch is going to get killed. But he takes the guy on, kicks him in the balls."

"That's what you did?"

"Swung from the heels. I missed."

She laughed, Alan joining her, her laughter deep and melodious as she turned back to the wall map. He watched her, his feelings for her surging. He tried to restrain them. He couldn't.

"Listen," he said, fighting the croak in his voice, "We got to talk."

"We're talking," she answered, her gaze locked on the map.

"I'm not quite sure how to say this…"

"Tongue River!" It came out of her like an explosion with a burst of realization. "The Tongue River Valley! The Battle of Wolf Mountain! It had to be! It was Crazy Horse's last fight! It was fought along the Tongue River! The fight was a draw, but it demonstrated the Sioux, Lakota and Cheyenne were no longer a match for the Army. That's when Crazy Horse surrendered!"

"The Tongue River," Alan repeated.

"You said in class Paythan was distressed that Crazy Horse surrendered,"

"That's what he said."

"The Tongue River's where it happened. That's where Paythan went."

"You don't know that."

"I don't know anything."

"What are you going to do?"

"I'm going to start there."

In his staff room, Police Chief Hurd sat back in his chair, put his feet up on the desk, fingers fluttering up and down on the arm of his chair as he stared at Maka and Alan seated across from him. Alan stared at the Chief's boots for a moment admiring the craftsmanship and detail put into the unique designs stitched into the boots.

"You know you shouldn't have jurisdiction there," he told Maka.

"Maybe," she said.

"Your authority is not this reservation anymore."

"It is, now." She showed him her U.S. Marshal badge. Last the Chief knew she left the reservation to join the F.B.I. He hadn't heard she had been recruited into the Marshals, which was Maka's dream all along. She knew she could have more of an impact as a Marshal than any other agency on the reservation.

"What the hell are you thinking?"

"I'm thinking somebody there murdered one of our people."

"The American authorities."

"Tried that."

Hurd turned to Alan. "Where are you in this?"

Alan opened his mouth to reply when his cell phone went off. Retrieving it from his pocket, he glanced to see who was calling.

"Excuse me," he said, rose, and sought a corner of the room. "Hey, Jer," he said into the phone.

"Where are you? NBC's been trying to get hold of you since yesterday."

"South Dakota."

"Very funny."

"Funny is as funny does."

"Where are you, God damnit!"

"Trying to track down the killers of one of my students."

"That's what you want me to tell 'em?"

"Tell them this. I'm on an Indian reservation researching Hutton: Annie Get Your Gun. There's a song in it, *I'm an Indian Too.*"

"You want me to tell them *that?*"

"Works for me."

"If I don't pull it off, you'll never work in his town again."

"Hey," Alan replied, on edge. "That's why you get the big bucks."

"You're giving me a heart attack!"

"Jer, I don't know what else to tell you! Get a pacemaker!"

He disconnected the cell, immediately regretful at his flash of anger, and stood a moment. Pocketing the phone, he returned to Maka and Hurd, slid into his chair, sat a moment unspeaking. Both looked at him, awaiting his answer to Hurd's question.

"Can I have a glass of water?" he asked.

Hurd snapped his fingers toward one of his staff.

"Clare? Glass of water, please."

She brought it to Alan; he drank it and lowered it to the table.

"He saw what he thought was wrong," Alan said at length. "He wanted to right it. He hated the injustice of what happened to his people and went out to rectify it." He looked at Maka. "He paid with his life for that. I want to know by whom and why."

They were back in Maka's house, preparing to leave, bags packed for traveling, Alan's shoes a cause for delay.

"You can't get away with those shoes."

Alan looked down at his Guccis, already starting to fall apart.

"What'll I wear?

Leaving the living room, Maka went into the hall, opened the door to a closet, pulled out a plastic laundry basket filled with used, discarded shoes, and returned them to Alan.

"What are these?" Alan asked.

"Donated, discarded, collected for the super poor. See what you can find."

In four minutes, Alan had found a pair of size ten boots, battered but serviceable, and slipped them on. They fit.

"Credit cards, cash," Alan said, going through his wallet, then tucking it away in his pocket. "We're in business."

"Sit down for a minute," she said.

She sat at the large center table, Alan following, wondering if he was being too jovial. That wasn't it.

"We're going into Cheyenne territory," she said.

"The Tongue River Valley?"

"Cheyenne. They're very compatible with the Lakota. Fought with us against Custer. But they're shy. The last thing they want is to become a target for anyone's displeasure. We're there for one thing only, remember that. Did Paythan come through? That's it, that's all."

"No interviews," Alan answered. "Got it."

She looked at him. Was he being sarcastic or genuine? She thought she detected a touch of irritation in his tone.

"It's about three hours," she said. "Gas up then we go."

The drive through and off the Pine Ridge reservation along a secondary highway into the Black Hills of lower southeast Montana was as predicted, three hours, into the center of the once Lakota and Cheyenne world, and the birthplace of Crazy Horse. Immediately it was an immensely different topography. Timbered ridges of pine hills. Buttes, alternating with grasslands of alfalfa, barley, and corn, along with miles of oddly shaped ridges, cliffs, and cones. Maka and Alan crossing the Tongue River by mid-afternoon. Coming to the Tongue River Agency, home to several hundred Cheyenne of the five thousand that currently occupied the entire reservation. They passed the schoolhouse, store buildings, blacksmith and carpenter shops, coming at length to the one-story Agency Office.

Sitting for a moment, staring out at the river, at the surrounding hills, ripe with mountain alder, Canterbury bells, and golden clover, Alan could only shake his head in awe.

"God," he said.

"God what?" Maka asked.

"What they had here."

The interior of the Agency Office was one room, void of secretarial staff. There was a desk, an out-of-date computer, a phone, and little else, other than two men, Cheyenne elders, already present, as their apparent leader, White Hawk, led in Maka and Alan. With greying hair and a noticeable limp from a long-ago battle with a diamondback, he wore the snake's rattlers around his neck.

"Esto'eohtse!" White Hawk said in Cheyenne as Maka and Alan followed. "Come! Come in!" Then, by way of introduction, "Grey Wolf, Spotted Elk!"

The other two, though younger, captured Alan's immediate attention. Almond-shaped, almost Asian looking eyes, Alan saw large front teeth with more than a slight gap. Physically, they seemed to be built with an almost inverted breastbone. The term "Red Indian" he quickly realized was a misnomer. Their hue was dark, approaching chocolate, due mostly to a lifetime of exposure to the elements. Their hair was straight, slightly coarser than the average white, abundant, and long.

"We think there was a boy who came through here," Maka began in English as she entered. "A Lakota. We have some questions."

"Nohtsesta ma'aataemeo'o," Grey Wolf said. Maka shook her head. "I don't understand."

"He wants to know about the railroad."

"What railroad?"

"Ho'no ev ma'aataemso'o," White Hawk answered Grey Wolf. "Ae hovahese… (This is not about the railroad. They come to…)"

"Pono hto! (Useless!)," said, Grey Wolf.

"Nona'so'eests! (Waste!")" added Spotted Elk, and the two men left the room. White Hawk spread his hands wide with a shrug. "The Tongue River Company," he explained, "wants an eighty-mile rail line along the river, digging coal mines. We don't want a coal train to destroy the valley. Everyone's upset. They thought you might be here for that."

"I'm sorry. I'd like to have spoken to them if they spoke English."

"Oh, they speak English," White Hawk said, then, "Here," he said, leading them to a couch that looked like it had been rescued from a rummage sale.

"We're trying to investigate a murder," Maka said as they sat. "Who did it and why?"

"A Lakota boy, you said," White Hawk acknowledged.

"I was his teacher at college in California…" Alan started to speak.

"They found his body in Mexico," Maka interrupted, making clear she would do the talking, "beaten to death, which, we think, is the last place he would have gone on his own."

"We heard of it," White Hawk acknowledged.

"His name was Paythan," Maka continued. "Paythan Burke. He was infatuated with Crazy Horse, but not with the great leader's surrender, which emanated…"

"Emanated?" White Hawk shook his head, not understanding the word.

"…began," Maka simplified the meaning, "from this place. We think Paythan may have come here in search of answers, or to accomplish a different ending."

White Hawk, who had not followed Alan and Maka to the couch, sank onto a packing box across from them.

"What different ending?"

Maka glanced at Alan, then back at White Hawk.

"Was he here?" she said. "That's what we want to know. He was upset that Crazy Horse surrendered to the long rifles and lost the Black Hills. We think Paythan may have wanted to start the war again."

"Penahe!" White Hawk blurted out in Cheyenne. "Insane! Where does he come to such a thing?"

"Crazy Horse," Maka answered.

White Hawk threw his head back in distress and dropped it to his chest in resignation.

"He was here," he said at length. "Paythan?"

"Paythan," Maka answered.

"He came with four others on horses. They camped by the river, two days. Young, eighteen to twenty. I went to talk to them, to see if they needed anything, like directions. One did the talking. He didn't speak Cheyenne, but his English was so good."

"Paythan," Alan confirmed.

"He asked what a lot of the young ones always asked. Why did Crazy Horse surrender after Little Big Horn? All seemed satisfied with the answer. Not Paythan. He said Crazy Horse should have known the government could not be trusted when it promised the Black Hills to us then broke that promise. I could see his anger; he wasn't the first. One of the other boys said they went to the protest, Paythan would not let him say anything more. When he left, I thought no more of it 'til I heard he was killed in Mexico."

Maka thought for a minute.

"Did he say where he was going from here?" she asked.

"He asked more questions than he gave answers," White Hawk replied. "When he left, they went north."

"Why north?" Alan asked.

"The reservation runs north," Maka answered. "I think he was looking for something."

"Or someone," Alan added.

White Hawk thought about that, shook his head in dismay.

"Man camps are north. Fool's dream. Did you ask his sister?"

Alan looks at Maka, "I reached out to her, went to her house and no one has seen her since the protest. Her aunt told us she went to the protest with some of her friends and Paythan. I assumed she was still off with her friends. I was hoping we would find some information to help us."

White Hawk seemed surprised by her answer. "I heard they had a run-in with those skinheads. I was sure she went home. People seem to disappear easily here," he said.

"We're going to try to follow his trail," Maka said. "But we'll need a place for the night."

"There's nothing on the reservation," White Hawk said. "Twenty miles up there's a crossing off the reservation to State Twenty. That'll take you to some inns and diners. That is where a lot of the protestors stayed, so I heard."

Napčíyuŋka

9

The Black Bear Inn, a two-story bed and breakfast, was located in the south-western Black Hills on State 20, across the street from a fast-food diner.

Turning off the highway into the parking area, Maka slowed her Wrangler for the yardman raking leaves off the drive-in entrance. Dressed in coveralls, he was about forty, swarthy, hair drawn back in a single pig-tail. Alan had not been in the area long enough to know his tribe.

"Cheyenne," Maka translated for him, reading the look on his face as she drove up to the front of the building and stopped. The inn, they noticed, was virtually unoccupied. There was a single pickup in the park-ing area and a sign above the entrance reading "Vacancies Available."

Leaving Maka's car, they gathered their overnights, climbed the stairs to the entrance, and entered.

The inn's lobby was standard, with no one currently on duty at the desk, but hostility greeted them in the form of three white men lounging in wicker chairs off the entrance. Aged twenty to twenty-five, they were of a kind. Shaved heads except for one with a Mohawk, steel-toed combat boots, bomber jackets, neo-Nazi, spider web, and power tattoos on their necks and heads, one with a swastika carved into the side of his, another with an anarchy sign, "Hammer Skin Nation" emblazoned across their T-shirts. The one with the Mohawk was the sole one in movement. An eight-inch stick fluttered back and forth through the fingers of his right hand as he took measure of Maka.

Crossing with Alan to the desk, Maka watched as Alan tapped the summoning bell. Seconds later, a young woman emerged from an inner office, a welcoming smile on her face.

"Hello," she greeted them cheerfully.

Alan returned her greeting with a smile.

"We'd like a couple of rooms for the night," he said.

"Wonderful," she said, turning the reservation calendar about. "We have two rooms I think you'd like, in the back facing the stream. It's sixty-five dollars a night for each roo…"

She stopped, seeing Maka. Her face seemed to freeze.

"Give me a moment, please," she said and disappeared into the room behind the counter. There was the sound of voices inside. A moment later an older man emerged and looked Maka over.

"Sorry," he said. "We're full up."

"You've got one car in the parking area," Alan said.

"It's the motorcycle rally in Cedar Rapids," the man explained. "We've been booked for two weeks."

Alan looked from the man to Maka. Her face was stone.

"Cedar Rapids is two hours from here," Alan said.

"We're booked," the man said.

"So, get out of our country" came a voice from behind.

Alan turned to the voice. It was the one with the Mohawk.

"Fuck your Indian whore somewhere else."

Rage welled up in Alan's face. He went for the skinhead, recoiled as the Mohawk flipped open a switchblade knife, and just as quickly dropped the blade and the eight-inch stick to the floor, threw his hands in the air as he faced Maka, Glock service automatic in her hand, aimed at his chest.

"On the floor, on your knees, hands behind your head!"

It was said with such authority, there was no questioning the order. The skinhead did as he was told, slumped to the floor on his knees, hands behind his head, his two companions shrinking back in their chairs. Maka turned to the proprietor standing shocked behind his desk.

"Who has authority here?" Maka said to the man who stood frozen. "*Who?*" She demanded.

"Highway Patrol," he answered.

"Call them!"

Ten minutes later a white highway patrol with an identifying black stripe running along its side, pulled into the parking lot. A uniformed officer emerged. He was a large man, slightly overweight, late fifties, used to dealing mostly with drunks and bent fenders. What he encountered when he entered was not the usual. Still on the floor, on his knees, was the skinhead with the Mohawk, still under Maka's Glock. At the patrolman's entrance, the skinheads cut loose.

"Shit, man! We're minding our own! This fucking squaw!"

"One at a time!" The officer turned to Maka. "You first."

"We came to check in…" Alan starts to explain.

"I said her," the officer said.

"We were trying to check in," Maka explained, then nodded at the switchblade on the floor. "He pulled that."

"Bull shit!" the Mohawk whined, then glared at Alan. "That ass hole was coming…!"

"Shut up!" the officer said, then turning back to Maka, "And you are?"

Her free hand dug into her purse, pulled out her wallet, flipped it open, and handed it to the officer who took it and stared at it with genuine surprise. The officer turned to the skinheads.

"What're you guys doing here?"

"We're staying here," the Mohawk answered.

The officer turned to the proprietor. "That true?"

"Checked in."

"Cash or credit card?"

"Credit."

"Void the reservation." Then turning to the skinheads, "Get out of here."

"Fuck you!" Mohawk replied.

Seeing the officer reach for his cell phone, the skinheads chose the wiser course and rose to leave. Passing Alan, Mohawk tossed a warning.

"I wouldn't sleep if I was you," he said and led the other two out the door.

When they were gone, the officer handed Maka's wallet back to her. "I have to ask, Marshal…"

"We're tracing a murder," Maka said. "We think the victim was in this area before his death."

He was young, about twenty. Lakota. His name was Paythan Burke. We think he was trying to recreate Crazy Horse or something."

"You're kidding."

"I wish I were. Meanwhile, we need someplace to stay for the night."

The officer looked at the proprietor who'd been standing by incredulously.

"I got a business to run," he said almost with a sense of apology.

The officer looked back at Maka and Alan. "You're going to run into the same thing up and down the corridor."

Maka had spent her life absorbing racism and shrugging it off, which was how you dealt with it.

"Thanks for the heads up," Alan said.

The officer looked Alan over. "You're from?"

"L.A.," Alan answered.

"Slumming?"

"Research."

"Dodger fan?"

"When they're winning."

"I got a son," the officer said, "Single A ball. Pioneer League."

"Like everybody else," Alan said.

The officer grinned and nodded at the reality of it all.

"What about those three?" Alan asked.

"Skinheads," the officer answered. "Nothing to mess with. They're nasty fascist racists. Like a fifth column up here. If you encounter their like again give them a wide berth."

Alan nodded. "Got it. Thank you."

The officer glanced at the proprietor and saw there was nothing further to negotiate. He turned to the door.

"Luck," he said and was gone.

Alan drew in his breath, exhaled, picked up their overnights, and looked back for Maka; she wasn't following. She was staring at what appeared to be the switchblade on the floor. It wasn't the knife that held her interest. Settling onto her heels, she reached down and picked up the wooden twig. Eight to ten inches long, with meticulously shaved ends, it was identical to the ones she and Alan had found at the Whispering Cedar Cemetery.

In the parking lot, in her Wrangler, Maka hunched behind the wheel, and next to her sat Alan, the two of them staring into the late day, wondering what next when a Suzuki Boulevard motorcycle pulled up beside the driver's side window. Astride it was the Cheyenne yardman. With a nod, he indicated they were to follow.

An hour and a half later, daylight faded, they found themselves re-crossing the Tongue River, reentering a portion of what remained of the Cheyenne reservation, thirty miles north of where they'd been earlier at the Tongue River Agency.

What used to be a three-to-four-acre reservation had been reduced by half. Several old dirt lodges still stood, most abandoned, dilapidated from stages of decay. Built-in circular form, fifteen to twenty feet in diameter, only a dozen lodges were still habitable. Among the larger ones still standing were smaller ones, made of roughhewn wood; for old people living alone, or used as menstrual lodges, or even for dogs.

Pulling to a stop before the larger of the structures, the yardman dismounted and indicated that Maka and Alan were to follow him inside. He walked through the deteriorating hallway, lined with doors to about six rooms. Some of the numbers on the doors missing, some swinging by one nail. Alan and Maka follow him to a room with a desk, he fumbled on the desk through paperwork and looked around the room. He took two keys off a hook on the wall. The keychains had numbers on them, room numbers. He handed one key to each of them.

Alan, uncomfortable with the silence, cleared his throat and began to try and speak "Thank you, how…" Maka gently kicked his shoe with hers to stop him from speaking. She nudged Alan in the side with her elbow, the yardman just stood in silence, emotionless. Maka nodded her head in gratitude and started to walk back down the hallway. Alan nodded his head toward the yardman and followed Maka.

Alan wanted to ask her what that was all about but her energy and lack of attention towards him indicated she wanted to be left alone. He respected that and when she approached her door Alan stepped behind her, reaching over to help her unlock the door, his chest pressed into her back, she leaned into him. The silence seemed to close in on them, so much so that all Alan could do was feel a deep breath she took when she leaned back and he felt the pounding of his heart against her. He turned the doorknob, pushing the door open slowly.

Maka pressed back a little more, holding her breath, and began to reach for the doorknob, placing her hand on his. She turned slowly and their eyes locked. Their faces were so close that Alan could feel her breath against his cheek. She smelled incredible. He gently removed his hand from the doorknob, and as he brought it back to his side, he brushed against her waist.

Maka took a small step backward into the room, keeping her hand on the door the entire time. Alan was pulsating from head to toe, he found himself speechless. He didn't want to break eye contact as Maka slowly stepped into the room, closing the door between them. She smiled a small smile and said "good night" as the door closed on Alan.

Maka tossed her bag onto the bed, looking around the outdated room, mattress visibly sunk in the middle, the wallpaper stained yellow from tobacco and water damage, a cockroach crawled quickly under the nightstand. She tried to close the curtains, but they were so old they began to fall apart. She gave up and looked over at her bag, abandoned on the bed. She worked her way over and shuffled through her bag, pulling out the file folders from Paythan's case. She started to arrange the documents and photos across the bed, studying them carefully as she placed each one down. Papers and photos were covering the Cheyenne printed blanket on the sunken mattress. Maka studied the collage looking for a different perspective. "Talk to me Paythan, what were you doing in Tijuana?" Maka asked out loud. Grabbing a yellow envelope, she shook it to make sure it was empty, a piece of paper fell out.

"I don't remember seeing this before", picking it up Maka continued talking to herself. "Hmmm? in Spanish, great."

Something in one of the photos caught her eye, she leaned over to get a closer look. In the photo of Paythan's body, lying next to a river, she could see headlights from a highway off in the distance. Studying it, she walked closer to the lamp on the nightstand. There was a person in the background. She could see the figure, but not in great detail. It appeared ghostly, there was something familiar about the figure. Looking even closer, there was an oddly shaped mark on Paythan's wrist. Maka spoke to herself, pondering the evidence scattered across the bed. There were photos of pieces of clothing in plastic bags that were saturated in blood.

She knew something was off with this as well, could someone be tampering with the evidence? Why? She began to pace, thinking they never put evidence in plastic bags, that's made for movies. It's supposed to be kept in brown paper bags, or boxes.

Moments later, Alan's room was dark with only the glow from the bathroom illuminating the bed and an old table and nightstand. He walked out of his bathroom, towel wrapped around his waist, brushing his teeth. There was a quick knock at his door. The room was so small he didn't have far to go, yet he somehow stubbed his toe on the way. "Shit! That hurt!" He hesitated to open the door, "Who is it?"

"It's me. Who else would it be in the middle of the night?" Maka answered.

Alan felt a bit silly; she made a good point. He didn't know, he grew up in the middle of LA. It was his first time in the middle of nowhere on a murder investigation.

Alan opened the door, still babying his toe, toothbrush still in his mouth and now his towel was slipping. Maka quickly looked him over as she entered the room. She had so much excitement, more than Alan had seen on the trip. She quickly handed him a ticket she found, and started to pace back and forth, talking with her hands.

"Xosio night club red light district" Alan reads. "What is this from?"

"I found it in Paythan's belongings." Maka continued to pace.

"I had this thought, maybe I'm crazy for thinking this but what if Paythan wasn't really trying to re-create Crazy Horse? I found this on the floor at the last hotel." She showed Alan the stick. "It's identical to the ones you found at the cemetery." She continued to talk faster, excitement building. Alan couldn't do much more than just listen. "What if Paythan and his sister were reuniting? They were just hiding out someplace here on the reservation. But that wouldn't make sense, why would they hide?

What if Paythan stumbled across something more than the political battle for the Black Hills? I mean, the oil; the gold. The pipeline, man camps. There are so many layers. He had to have discovered something that someone didn't want anyone to know about. Right?"

She looked at Alan who still favored his foot and stood there motionless, holding the corner of his towel.

"What's wrong with your foot?" Alan attempted to answer her.

"Oh well, when I heard the knock…"

Maka interrupted him and went on saying "I started thinking about some of the evidence the department had and how it doesn't line up. How did they end up here? Why would they come here? As soon as there is light, I want to walk by the river in the morning." She looked over at the old digital clock on the nightstand, which said 2:22 a.m.

Someplace in the pacing and rambling Alan found himself getting lost in his thoughts, observing this exuberant woman, full of life. Suddenly he found himself seeing her differently than the assertive tomboy. The energy she was exuding sparked a memory for him, something he wrote once as a scene in one of his movies. He played it over in his head as that took precedence and her voice became background music to his ears. He recalled, 'a proper kiss…'

Back her up against the wall, use your knees to spread her thighs. Now press your thigh against her. Grab her wrists with one hand and hold them above her head. Brush her hair from her face. Lift her chin until your eyes meet. Look her intently in the eyes as if you desire to devour her. Lean in closely. Wait for her to close her eyes. Then, and only then, brush your lips against hers. Let your tongue find hers. Never break the kiss first. 'That is how you kiss a woman.'

Maka stopped speaking, breaking Alan's trance. As fast as their eyes connected, Maka broke the connection.

Alan moved in close enough to feel the body heat radiating from her chest, "You're pretty cute when you get excited," he whispered in her ear. He reached out to touch her face, brushing her long, black silky hair away from her eyes, he gently let it settle behind her ear. Never breaking eye contact, she pressed her cheek to his hand. She took a deep breath and so did he.

He didn't know what to do next, he had never felt this kind of connection with anyone before. He was mesmerized as he lost himself in the energy that was emanating from their bodies being this close. His knees trembled, and Maka placed her hand on Alan's as she ran her fingers softly up his arm. They both felt the same way; like it was their very first time.

Alan dropped the corner of his towel as he gently grabbed her slender waist. He placed his thumb at the small of her back, tracing the top of her jeans around, and paused at the button. She trembled; not because it tickled but from the sensuality of his touch. Without thinking, she stepped in closer, and Alan's towel dropped to his feet.

Maka could not break away from the intense look in Alan's eyes. It's as if their souls became one as they pressed in to get even closer. He leaned down gently kissing her forehead. He savored the earth scent that excited him earlier, he gently kissed the corner of each piercing eye. The sensation was intense, and he meant to soak up every moment. He traced his lips across her cheek, as he moved in closer to the nape of her neck. He couldn't stop his hands from running over her delicate shoulders, down her arms, and around her smooth stomach, anticipating the moment that he would reach up to touch her perky breasts. He fluttered his lips across her neck until he found her lips with such passion that she can barely breathe.

As their excitement grew, so did the intensity of their kiss. Neither one of them had felt this much passion before. She could feel his manhood grow as he pressed against her. He lifted the bottom of her shirt, and she complied by raising her arms as he lifted it over her head. His eyes followed the silhouette of the curves of her toned body illuminated by the glow of the bathroom light. He moved to unbutton her jeans, turning her back toward the bed, he gently slid her pants down as she laid back on the bed. Like a dance, they flowed in sync with one another, as if it had been choreographed just for them. He caressed her feet, running his hands along her calf, up and around her thigh, he placed his lips behind her knee, as she arched her back. He reached up to her white lace panties as he savored the roundness of her hips. Gently kissing her inner thigh, he lowered her panties exposing the folds of her velvety sex. He could barely wait for his first sweet taste as he glided her panties around her ankles.

Thoughts flooded through Maka's mind; she had never been touched like this before. His touch went beyond the flesh, into the depths of her inner being. The intense passion was building within her, growing with every kiss, and with every touch of his hand. She wondered for a moment if this was what love felt like. Real love. She battled with old thoughts as painful memories tried to surface, though the weight of his body brought her back to the present moment and she once again felt the intensity and energy as he peered into her eyes. Time and space lost all meaning.

Maka ran her fingers through the hair on the back of his head, her hands settling on his sculpted shoulders. His lower back arched and the embrace intertwined them as their bodies and souls rhythmically became one. Mirroring each other's actions, it was as if they were molded to fit each other. Breathing more heavily, she wrapped her legs around his waist and pressed her breasts against his chest as their bodies continued to merge. He took his time, and he effortlessly glided inside her. Her back arched in response, pressing herself up against him. He penetrated the very depths of her being, and he completely surrendered himself into her. This was more than just sex.

They both felt the deepness of the union, as if their souls had been waiting for each other. They instinctively knew that they had been here before, maybe in another life; but the connection of their souls in that present moment was real. Many people may go a lifetime without meeting their soulmate. They were the lucky ones; their connection was truly spiritual.

Wikčémna

10

Morning arrived faster than either of them anticipated, Maka already outside for her morning prayer. Alan looked out the window and saw her off in the distance. As the sun rose the rays bounced off her black, silky hair, a beautiful soulful glow illuminated her. She appeared to be meditating or praying. He could faintly hear her singing or maybe chanting in her native language. He decided to give her time.

Alan reached into his bag and took out his laptop.

An email from Jerry, *"The studio is going to cancel your contract if you don't get your screenplay in by the end date. They mean it Alan, don't mess this up."*

He leaned back on the bed and began working on his screenplay. Maka began to walk around thinking about how wonderful the night with Alan was and then she started to talk herself out of having any feelings for him. She thought to herself, *My relationships never work out. I'm the job. It could never work out, we are from two different worlds; he is in a world of fiction, and I am in the disturbing reality of it. But we had such a beautiful connection, I've never had that with anyone before.* She had always dreamt to find her soul match, that person who would be a wonderful growth partner, that person she could share a life with and grow old together. More than a best friend, a connection deeper than any other, a safe place to just be, the one person she could trust more than anyone.

She continued to tell herself, *I've done the impossible. I earned where I am in a male-dominated world. I am vested. Not every female can meet that challenge.* She looked back and reminisced at moments when she faced negativity and struggled to balance her job with her personal life, reflecting on how much personal time she had to sacrifice to get the job done. Being strong-minded, very motivated, and passionate about the job helped her with the load and stresses of it all. She reminded herself that keeping her mind, body, and spirit aligned was what kept her a whole person. As she stopped to say a prayer in her native language, she noticed a loan wolf off in the distance watching her. The wolf is highly respected in by First Nations because of their likeness as a very family-oriented animal. The wolf represents loyalty, family, healing, protection and intelligence. The symbol and spirit of the wolf is very important to her and her culture. She gives thanks to the wolf for coming to her.

Unbeknownst, the yardman watched Maka from a distance.

Alan decided to join her, approaching slowly, smiling. Their eyes revealing their connection from their night together was still strong. "Good morning." Alan took her hand kissing the back of it, pulling her in gently, embarrassing her, and kissing her. Maka reciprocated, and pulled back.

"Good Morning. I hope I didn't wake you."

"No, I wish you would have." His smile revealed the little boy that still lived inside him. "I hope I'm not interrupting."

"Not at all. Are you a praying man Alan?"

"Well, not as much these days it seems. I need to be."

Maka sensed they were being watched and was right. She could see the yardman tucked in the corner of a shadow next to one of the old, dilapidated buildings.

"Did you just wake up?"

"No, I was working on my screenplay. My agent reminded me that my deadline is coming fast."

"You haven't mentioned a whole lot about it. What's it about?"

"An old-time actress, Betty Hutton. Her life was referred to as a dark roller coaster ride. She lost her father to suicide, she had a drinking problem and a breakdown. She was best known for *Annie's Got a Gun*."

"Oh, a movie star story."

Alan could see she seemed distracted and not very interested.

"Have you found anything?" Alan asked.

Maka turned and pointed to the river. Off in the distance a small band of horses crossed, "There might be a chance that Paythan and his friends were following the river."

They walked toward the river, taking in the soft breeze, a gentle whisper, and the sound of the ripples flowing through the water. "Tell me more about this area, Maka."

"What would you like to know?" Alan walked closer to the edge of the river to sit down and started to untie his boots.

"What are you doing?"

Alan slipped off his socks, "I was going to test the river."

"It's cold. Besides, you can't… it's polluted."

Alan stopped shy of placing a foot in the water. "What do you mean?"

"Several years ago, they allowed cattle ranchers to come. All the waste from the cattle was dumped into the river. They noticed after the children went swimming, they would develop sores and boils on their bodies." Maka bent down, and picked up a few rocks, skipping them into the river.

"I thought this was part of your water supply?" Alan put his boots back on.

"It is and there is a natural spring, one of the healthiest springs in the country, and they will not allow us to tap into it."

Alan stood, "Who won't?"

"Who do you think?" Maka responded hastily.

The two of them walked along the river, Maka continued to respond to his questions.

"Our reservation has become like a third-world country. We are a spiritual people, there are four aspects of who we are: our mind, heart, body, and spirit. Many people here have given up, they have tried to disenfranchise the families."

Alan reached for Maka's hand and continued to walk. She was relieved to have someone who cares to hear her story. Maka went on to explain, "The White Buffalo Calf Woman is our cultural prophet. She brought the 'Seven Sacred Rules' by which we live. When the Catholic churches opened the boarding schools, at first, they would steal the children to put them in the schools, then the parents had to surrender their children or go to jail. Once in the boarding schools the nuns would cut their hair, which is important in our culture. The only time we cut our hair is when someone close to us dies. When they cut the children's hair, many of them ran away to come home... if they lived to make it home. Many times they suffered from frostbite, lost a leg, and some died." Maka paused a moment as they watched the herd of wild horses graze in front of them. Taking a deep breath she continued. "The church wiped the children's identity. Forced them to wear uniforms, changed their diet, abused them, and tried to kill their spirit. The whole system tried to erase us. The killing of millions of our people from years ago still lives in our DNA, and we can feel it. When you take the language, food source, a way of life, from a people, that's genocide. Now there is a disconnect and you can see it, where they hurt. Now the people are fighting gang violence, domestic calls, sexual abuse and poverty. It's sad because I know our ancestors didn't pray for any of this."

Alan listened intently; he wanted to ask more questions but stopped himself from interrupting. He reflected on how closed off she had been, understanding that probably came with the job. She had trust issues, rightfully so. He could see under that protective armor she had built around her; underneath she was still a girl who had so much love to give but hadn't found a safe place to give it. He could see the pain she used to fuel her efforts in her career, having to work in some of the darkest places that an average person never saw or even knew existed.

Maka went on to share, "My grandma raised fourteen of us in a five-bedroom house, she did everything for us, cooked, cleaned, and took care of us."

She was feeling too vulnerable, so she stopped herself from going any deeper into her past, and grabbed his hand, changing the subject. "It is too hard to ignore the human cost of what we are doing. I want to check out all the buildings up the road. Do you want to come with me?"

Looking back to the lodge and then up the road, pondering on whether he should work on his screenplay or go with Maka, Alan said, "Of course, I will come with you."

Maka was leading them to the structure. Alan was still lost in his thoughts from their night together, watching her walk through the field of golden grass in some areas higher than their knees, a gentle breeze whisps through her black silky hair reflecting the morning sun.

What seemed to once have been a beautiful flower garden was now just a hostile of weeds and thorn bushes. The dilapidated building had visible holes in the roof, the wood was weathered, windows were broken, and some were boarded as if it was left to die here, alone, as if no one cared. She approached cautiously. The deeper they stepped in, the more vulnerable Maka felt they were. There was no door, the entryway seemed monstrously massive.

"Watch your step, the floorboards could be rotted out." Alan nodded, and he allowed Maka to lead them.

"People live or lived in here?" he asked. Maka brushed away cobwebs.

"Yes, the poverty rate is much higher on reservations than it is nationally. It's something around thirty-six percent of families are below poverty compared to nine percent nationally."

Entering deeper, an old rusty wheelchair covered in dust sat in one corner. There were many rooms, a kitchen with old, stained dishes, a common area, and a warped desk in the corner with stacks of paper and garbage on the floor. But it hadn't been occupied in a very long time. Maka didn't feel they were in the right place.

"Nothing." She led Alan out a back door.

A few football fields away was another big housing structure.

"I'm speechless," Alan said. "I would have never imagined the reservation would look or feel this way. You see pictures and read stories, but to be standing in the middle of it all. The natural beauty that surrounds this depressed, third-world desolation, that is supposed to be a community. As I look into the eyes of the people, I can see, generationally, their humanity was taken away from them. Right here in our own backyard. I'm sorry Maka, I'm speechless. I noticed the only building that had electricity is the one we stayed in, and it is rigged together with extension cords."

Maka's presence became more stoic, "Most of the Res does not have electricity or Wi-Fi. This is one of the few spots that has it." Trying to stay on task, Maka knew there was an old farmhouse about a mile up the road. "Let's grab our things and head out, there are a couple more places I need to check out."

Maka saw the yardman off in the distance, standing next to his truck, watching. They walked back to get their things. Alan was getting edgy, not knowing what they were doing or what was expected of him. His personal feelings for her were what helped him to push past feeling estranged in her world.

Driving down the rough, jarring road neither said much to the other. Alan was taking in the scenery and wondering why these structures were abandoned. Maka turned into what once looked like a driveway. Tire tracks were indented in the grass that overtook it, indicating that it had been used recently. Approaching a makeshift gate that was padlocked, she had to park and leave her Jeep there.

"You can wait here if you want. I won't be long."

They both got out of the jeep; she walked up ahead a few steps, bending down to take a closer look at the tire tracks.

"Appears someone has been here recently."

"How can you tell when someone was here recently? I see the grass pressed down but it could have been months ago?"

"Not necessarily. See the grass is still laying down, there is no new growth, and there is some scat from deer that is fresh."

Alan was intrigued.

"Ok. How do you know this stuff?"

"Tracking comes kind of naturally, I guess. It's something I grew up with on the res. And I was lucky enough to work a case with the Shadow Wolves."

Maka walked around the gated area, observing, looking for clues or anything that might help.

"What's a shadow wolf?" Alan imagined it was some kind of pack of wolves.

"You've never heard of them? Of course, not."

"No."

"They do keep their organization quiet. So, it's an extension of ICE. Only Native American men and women agents. It's composed of limited members of tribes like the Sioux, Navajo, Lakota, Tohono O'odham, plus a few other tribes working the borders, mostly in Arizona."

They continued to walk; Maka checked the area closest to the gate.

"They look for stories written on the ground."

"Special training?"

"Only by the elders, to hear things that are silent and to see invisible things. It can seem uncanny at times when you walk with the elders."

"Interesting, I would love to experience that one day."

Maka crossed in between the barbwire fence, her shirt snagging just a bit.

"I'm going to check out the house. It would be so helpful if you walk the fence and see if you find anything like clothing, cigarettes, or a piece of gum. Anything that you might feel shouldn't be there. Take a picture with your phone and mark it with a stick. If anything happens, if anyone comes, I want you to get in the Jeep and lock the doors. If you need help, lay on the horn: the 9mm is under the passenger seat."

Alan started to feel a little uneasy now. At first, he stood back and wondered why she trusted him to find anything. Then he felt moved that she trusted him enough to look for her. Now she was telling him there could be something that endangered his life. He scratched his head and thought, *Lord, what am I doing here?* He looked around the area.

Maka felt better if Alan stayed close to the car. She felt it was safer for him to be there not knowing what she might be walking into.

She walked through the tall golden grass, and off in the distant mountains formed a silhouette behind the rolling hills. Alan watched as she took tenuous steps towards the house, she was very cautious, observing the surroundings. He thought to himself, *She keeps getting more and more interesting... Shadow Wolves. What next?*

She reached the house. She hesitated, looking both ways instead of walking onto the porch and going in the front door. Something tugged at her intuition, telling her to go around to the rear of the building. The more she walked around the more it appeared inhabitable on the outside. A few old, abandoned cars and trucks with their windows broken, one partially stripped, were parked around the house. As she got to the back of the house, the long weeds seemed to have been trampled down in some areas. Tire tracks were leading up to the back porch.

The exterior paint was chipping on the side of the house, and shingles were missing from the roof. She walked up three steps to the back door.

She turned the doorknob; it opened right away. It was dark inside, with only a little natural light peaking in through the small windows of the building. As she stepped further into the house, she noticed a stench that grew stronger, curling the hairs on her arm. Not only was it musky and damp, but the house felt stale, and heavy energy lingered. She started coughing; the lifted floorboards made an eerie creaking sound as a light breeze whistled through the window.

Maka continued to explore, dusty old furniture scattered around the house had a pungent odor. A torn oversized chair, threads hanging from the armrests, an antique coffee table covered with old papers, and empty food containers. The kitchen sink was filled with rotting food and old-dishes. She walked through the hallway and up the stairs. There were several bedrooms, observing each of them as she passed, one had an old baby crib in the corner of the room, and the other had a twin-size mattress on the floor with a stained sheet. Maka stepped into the hallway and took a deep breath, she was sure that there would be a clue here.

She heard a vehicle pulling up and began making her way back to the first floor. She started to walk towards the back entrance and noticed another door she didn't see earlier. She cautiously opened it. The room was pitch black inside. She felt a pit in her stomach, nervously turned on the flashlight on her cell phone, and pointed it straight into the darkness. She looked behind her, no sign of Alan, and she didn't want to wait. Beginning her descent she found stairs, her flashlight barely illuminating the way. She recalled hearing squatters sometimes live in these abandoned houses.

She decided to walk down the stairs, one hand on her sidearm, the other gripping her phone. The stairs make a hollow sound every time she stepped down, she noticed odd scratch marks on the side of the walls, similar to that of a cat scratch or claw marks. Her light bounced off something that shined on the step, she got a closer look. It was a human fingernail, woman's, manicured, red nail polish, gel kind. She pulled a tissue from her pocket and picked it up with the tissue, folded it and put it in her pocket.

Reaching the bottom, the floor was partially dirt and old cement, more like a cellar than a basement. The ceiling was low and the smell a hundred times worse than upstairs.

Maka whispered to herself; "Wow, smells like something died down here. There has to be a dead animal or something." She covered her nose and mouth the best she could with her shirt.

She shined her phone flashlight from right to left, listening for any movement. An awful stench radiated toward her as she walked in a particular direction. As she followed the smell she noticed rooms with no doors, one had a stained towel draped over it. She shined her light into each room, finding they were consistent in that they had cots on the floor, dirty sheets, and buckets in the corners that still had human feces in them. She shined her light on the floor and could see imprints from shoes and even bare feet. She could tell they had not been there very long, maybe a week old at best or less. An overpowering, indescribable smell grew. Maka put her arm over her mouth and nose. She felt pulled to enter the room finding a massive dead rat, it had been there for a while, which explained the stench. She noticed some unique scratches on the wall near the bolt. Similar to the ones going down the stairs, she took a picture, and the flash revealed a crinkled paper in the corner. Maka picked it up, but before she could look at it, she heard a creaking sound coming from the stairs. Standing up, pointing the flashlight to the ground. "Alan?" Maka says softly but sternly. No answer. She could hear boots walking against the dirt floor. Pulling out her Glock, releasing the safety, and tightening her grip she called out "Alan, is that you?" No answer as the footsteps drew closer.

Maka announced "Marshal. Identify yourself." Back against the wall, firearm raised, she put her phone in her back pocket, eyes adjusting to the dark. She saw a glow from what appeared to be a flashlight outside the room she was in.

A silhouette of a man appears in the doorway. "What the fuck are you doing in here!" She recognized the voice; the light revealed Chief Hurd, shinning his flashlight in her face. "What the hell are you doing in here? Mr. Hollywood is waiting for you outside!"

Maka saw that he was holding a 9mm in his right hand. "Chief what is all this?"

"This is nothing." He waved his gun for her to leave the room.

As she walked past him, she could smell tobacco and whiskey. There was an eerie silence as they walked up the stairs.

Approaching the back door Maka's eyes struggled to adjust to the light, and she observed the area. Alan was standing at the Jeep. The yardman's truck blocked it from behind.

Hurd was still behind her, he tried to make it clear demanding "Go back to your wasicu wichasa. How dare you bring that white man here?"

Maka looked at Hurd, "He is not my boyfriend. I want to know what all this is."

Hurd was getting angry. "I told you…" He stopped himself from blowing up.

He shifted his tone to a more calm, professional one.

"Just the gangs squatting, you know how they are. We thought the gate would deter them. Guess it's not working."

Back at the Jeep, Alan watched Maka walking taller than he remembered her, her hand on the butt of her gun. "I'm driving. Get in." Alan didn't question her, the look in her eyes was more than any words could have suggested. Her eyes pierced through the yardman's soul. If looks could have moved him and his truck, hers would have moved him many light-years away. He got back in his truck and moved it just enough for her to get out and speed off kicking up rocks and dirt.

The silence was almost deafening in the Jeep as they drove away.

"Did you find something?" Alan asked breaking the silence.

"I think Paythan stumbled across something more than a political war over the Black Hills." In the rearview mirror, she realized they were being followed. Trying not to worry Alan, she chose not to say anything to him.

"What do you mean? What did you find?"

Taking her phone from her back pocket, she pulled up the photos she took for a closer look.

"Can I help you?" Alan asked as she jerked the stirring wheel again.

"Can you tell me what's going on?"

"Well, we are being escorted off the res."

Maka saw the truck behind getting closer, she accelerated. Alan noticed the speedometer climbing quickly. "I don't know how much you know about the rival gangs, cartels, and skinheads. Pine Ridge is the melting pot for all of it. Everything from drugs, human trafficking, and the KKK. Human trafficking of American Indian women and children has turned into a pandemic."

"I'm not very familiar, haven't seen much about it on the news."

"You won't, media blacks it out. Native American stories are rarely covered."

Alan watched the truck gaining behind them, "Is this something we should be concerned about?"

"Potentially… Did Paythan ever talk about friends or family?"

"No. Not really, he was quiet and very private. I didn't know he had a sister until just the other day."

"Most of his writings were about Crazy Horse and getting back the land. He was very much an advocate for his people and what he believed in. I did notice he would get very impatient with me and others for not understanding his struggles. At the same time, I didn't know he had struggles."

She was frustrated, running her fingers through her hair, "It's not adding up. Hurd told us he saw Paythan and the other boys. If he was there for the protest, how did he end up along the river with the other boys? Was he looking for something or maybe someone? There are over two million acres of this reservation."

Alan took notice she was going 80 mph and climbing, "Did you notice the gas light is on?" Maka looked, "There is a gas station coming up. Looks like our escort left."

Alan picked up his cell phone and scrolled through emails. "Now that you mentioned it, Paythan did email me a couple of weeks before he was found."

"Do you still have it?"

Alan continued to search, "I believe I do; I'm looking." Several minutes passed but to Maka, it felt like hours. Alan blurted out "Here it is!"

"Read it to me!"

"Well, it isn't much, he replied to one of my last emails giving him feedback on his screenplay. When he didn't return to class, I did reach out to see if he was OK and told him he needed to submit a final draft. He responded, but only with "The white buffalo calf woman." I didn't understand what that meant. Wondered if it was the title of his project."

Maka glanced at Alan, "It's a story, legend speaks to the choices men face in life. Either to take the black road of arrogance and entitlement by dishonoring sacred life or show up in respect for Mother Earth, take the road to honor, practice sacred ceremonies and prayer, to become responsible men who defend, protect and respect."

Maka thought to herself, was Paythan still defending the land or someone?

As they pulled into the gas station, they noticed the big 'M' on the sign.

Alan got out to pump the gas. A few skinheads were hanging out around the entrance of the station. He checked his phone while the tank was filling and saw there was another message from Jerry.

"Alan where are you? They are getting impatient. The heads are talking that if you don't deliver those pages, you won't work again in this town. Call me!"

Alan called Jerry back only to get his voicemail, so he decided to leave a message.

"Jer, they told me I had four weeks to complete this project and I still have two and a half weeks left. Do they want it done good or fast? I'll call you later."

Distracted, Alan didn't realize the gas was overflowing at first. By the time he caught it, it was running down the side of the jeep. As he went to get something to clean it up, he passed a few of the men, overhearing a few of their comments about some Native American boys coming out of the station. Maka was inside the Jeep, taking a closer look at the pictures she took in the basement, she was zooming in on them to get a closer look.

Alan approached her window and tapped on it, she lowered it, "Would you like anything from inside? I'm going to grab a few things."

Maka, distracted by the photos, "Sure coffee'd be great." Alan was going to try and kiss her but didn't.

Shuffling through the pictures, she remembered the paper she found. Pulling it from her pocket, she unfolded the receipt. She could read most of it: Mountain Dew, chips, cigarettes; the date was fading but she could see the time was 9:36 pm.

Alan returned, handed Maka her coffee, and tossed his bag of snacks on the floor.

Maka looked up, "I need you to go back inside and ask the manager how long they keep their video recordings. I would go but they won't talk to me here."

Alan looked around at all the commotion going on around the parking lot.

Alan looked stunned, "So, just ask how long?" he clarified.

She sipped on her coffee, "Yes."

While Alan went back inside, Maka got out to grab her bag in the back. She fumbled through pulling out a folder, she sat back in the driver's seat. Keeping one eye on the store and the people in the area, she quickly went through 4 x 6 and 8 x 10 photos of Paythan's body. She reviewed the report that went with them.

Alan slid back in the Jeep. "They aren't very friendly in there. The clerk said it goes to a corporate cloud if the cameras are on and working."

Maka intensely reviewed the folder, "That is what I thought they would say. We need to go to Tijuana."

She picked up her phone and emailed her office asking them to get a copy of the footage from the gas station.

Alan was confused, "What is going on, what did you find in the house?"

Maka handed the receipt to Alan, "What's this?" looking it over he saw the 'M' logo just like the gas station they were at.

"Look at the date," Maka pointed to it on the receipt. "I know it's fading, but it looks like around the date of the protest."

Alan looked at the folder, he saw the explicit photos of Paythan's body after he was found. It was unimaginable, his body almost unrecognizable from the beating. Alan wasn't prepared to see such graphic pictures, it felt like a punch in the gut. With a lump in his throat, Alan looked at Maka and said, "We're going to Tijuana."

Akéwaŋži

11

The Wrangler kicked up dust down the long gravel road. Alan observed sporadic housing at least a mile apart or more. Maka felt she needed to get back to her roots for a bit to help find clarity, and her Auntie's house came to mind. She knew it was always a safe place to clear her mind and refocus. She often would take time off throughout the year from work when she wanted to disappear for a few days and do a spiritual journey and reconnect.

"We need to make a couple of stops before we leave."

Alan reached down and pulled out his mini pop tarts. "Would you like some?"

Maka took one look, "No thank you, ya know what they put in those things?"

Alan laughed, "Yeah, but it's road trip food," passing a sign that says Oglala Lakota County.

"You were telling me about your grandmother and her raising you. Where in the lineup are you?"

Maka kept her eyes firmly on the road, "Number thirteen. Grams was tired by the time she had me come live with her. Our grandmothers are a very important part of our culture. Back in the day, the women had the power to take away a man from leadership if he did something to violate the laws of our people, or put a man back into leadership."

Alan couldn't hold back anymore and had to ask, "Why do you think that changed?"

"That is another conversation for another day. But many believed we need to go back to our society's ways."

Alan put away his snacks, "That is interesting, I never knew that."

"People say we are old-fashioned, the truth is we have forgotten who we are because of mainstream's expectations of being like them. Even the educational system is geared to assimilate our people into their thinking patterns, even our tribal government is based on that. Some people are saying they don't want traditional government, and yet if we veer away from that, we lose ourselves as a tribal nation and lose who we are because we are not connected to our spirit."

They were driving past a long-barbed wire fence, a single red dress was hanging on it, waving in the wind, with no houses in sight, just tall golden grass dancing behind, a row of trees, and a silhouette of mountains. Alan couldn't resist and asked, "Why would someone hang a dress out here?"

Maka tried to explain, "A girl went missing a few months ago and they decided to follow this case to bring awareness to #reddressproject for missing and murdered indigenous girls that started in Canada. There they believe the color red calls to the spirits."

Maka had to slow down, as she came up on several young girls on horseback riding up ahead. As they got closer and passed them, they noticed they were wearing colors, some riding bareback, others had a blanket between them and the horse. Alan commented, "Those girls look at peace."

She responded "Horses respond to emotional energy. When you ride, your horse can feel everything you do. You and the horse are supposed to become one. They can make you face your truth. Might even humble you if he has to. When you're on the back of the horse you can feel free, connected to the world." Alan continued to observe the riders as they slowly passed by.

Maka pulled up to a stop sign. On the corner is a telephone post with signs on it: INDIAN TACOS #87 NORTH RIDGE $5 WITH POP, and another, SUPER NACHOS WITH POP $4.00 CALL TO ORDER.

Moments later they turned onto a long gravel driveway leading to a single-wide, manufactured home. It appeared it was white, with streaks of rusty orange, one of the more well-kept homes Alan had seen for miles.

"This shouldn't take too long; we will have internet here." Maka grabbed her bag and escorted Alan to the house. As they approached the front door, Alan observed the area. Maka seemed confident they were in a safe place. Maka climbed the stairs onto the small porch, she knocked once and walked in.

Alan respectfully was a few feet behind Maka, he decided to give her some space. As Alan walked to the end of the house, he could see a few young children running and playing in the large field. They seemed happy, laughing, and chasing one another.

Maka noticed Alan wasn't behind her, she called out to him, "Alan."

Maka could hear several women chatting in the kitchen, she made her way to be in view. She could hear their conversation. They were talking candidly about the war in 1973.

"She was part of that, she was down at Wounded Knee." One of the women said.

"I was a messenger. They said I should never talk about it. I made a vow to keep my mouth shut." She giggles.

Maka interrupted, "Then don't talk about it, Annie. We don't want to know."

A woman in her late sixties, not very athletic, dressed in a loose t-shirt and loose pants, wearing a colorful strand of beads around her neck, her black hair, with highlights of grey, pulled back, jumped up quickly, excited to see Maka.

"Speak for yourself, I want to know." The woman laughs, extending her arms to hug Maka. All the women sitting around the table were over sixty, some dressed in colors and traditional Native garments, wearing beads and one with a feather in her hair.

Maka reciprocated the hug, "Auntie."

Alan could hear the chatter as he stood in the living room area wondering where he should go. He walked slowly behind Maka, she turned and reached as she was going to grab his hand, and she stopped herself.

"Ladies this is Alan, he is a professor at USC and is helping me with my case."

The ladies study him, looking him up and down. He wondered what they might be thinking of this tall white man standing in their presence.

Auntie smiled and with welcoming eyes, "Nice to meet you, Alan, please sit, you might be more comfortable on the couch."

Maka made her way around the table of women who were the leaders in their community. Annie is almost ninety years young, all of five feet tall, and petite.

The woman looks at Alan, saying "Hiyotaka."

Alan, unsure of what she said, decided to follow her, Maka saw him and quickly translated. "Auntie invited you to come and sit." Alan nodded "Thank you," he walked over to sit on the sofa.

Maka tried to get on the internet. "Auntie, what is the WIFI password?" "Oh I can't remember it. I don't know why they make them so long." She came back in the room handing Maka an index card with the password on it.

"Philakhiya," Maka thanked Auntie. "Be greatful you finally got internet connection here. The rural communities are still struggling to get it. Auntie took back the piece of paper with the password and placed it back on the refrigerator. "Oh, it's not just her on the Res?" Maka stopped typing, "No, it's across the country."

Alan decided to take this opportunity to check his emails on his phone, just as he suspected, there were several from Jerry and the studio. He reluctantly clicked on them one by one, suspecting the types of communications he was going to receive. He now only had two weeks to complete the screenplay. After finding email after email from Jerry asking for the script, he reached over and pulled out his laptop.

"Maka, do you need me for anything? The studio is hounding me for the screenplay."

"No go ahead, get some work done. I'll book our flights."

Auntie is filling the table with snacks, and baking fry bread in the kitchen. The aroma of fresh bread increases Alan's appetite. She placed down some paper plates, "Maka, are you still working on that missing boy case?"

"Yes, but it took a turn that I didn't see coming. There is something more, Auntie, what do you make of this?" Maka pulled up the images she took at the graveyard with the shaved sticks that she found and then scrolled to the rooms in the basement that she took. Auntie sat down next to her and looked closely at the photos.

Her face emotionless, she studied the photos. Maka, typing on her computer, "Looks like someone left a trail." Auntie set the phone down.

"The signs left by the young man; he is leading you. Though physically he is not here, his spirit is still communicating with you. You need to listen."

Maka looked at Auntie.

Auntie continued to say "The Res is a hunting ground for predators more now than ever. And the cartel presence has been growing."

"Yes, I know," Maka said.

Auntie looked over at Maka's computer screen. It was open to a previous case she had been working on. There were pictures of a young girl and an APP. "Does that have something to do with the boy?" she pointed to the computer screen.

"No, Auntie. This is another case, it is never ending."

"Is the girl safe?"

"For now. She has been using one of those APP's, where the men start grooming these young girls. Ya know, starts off wanting to watch them do their homework or brush their hair and they pay them. Then they slowly lure them to meet, rape and pay them. Eventually some of the girls end up trafficked or forced into it."

"That's horrible. Why they are called predators." Auntie stood and started to walk back to the kitchen.

Maka starred at the screen for a moment reflecting on some of the girls from her cases. "If only more parents felt comfortable talking to their kids about this or even do their own research so they know the signs to look for."

A knock at the door. A woman let herself in. She was wearing a black uniform, a badge pinned on her chest, POLICE on the back of her jacket, and her black hair tied back. She saw Maka sitting at the table.

"Mithan wichoun," speaking in a Native language addressing "sister."

"Hello, sister." Though the women are not blood-related they are sisters in protecting their community.

"What are you doing here?" The officer looked at Alan as she spoke to Maka.

Alan was already feeling like an outsider, he tried to avoid eye contact. He found it better to try and stay as invisible as he could.

Maka thought she'd better introduce them, "Autumn Chaska this is Alan, he is helping me with the case."

Autumn tucked her thumbs in her utility belt, "Nice to meet you, Alan."

Alan stood as a gentleman would, "Nice to meet you." Maka walked back to the table.

Alan sat back down, replacing his laptop as he continued to work on his script, while the ladies continued preparing a meal in the kitchen.

Maka moved her folders and bag to make room for Autumn.

"Sit, I want your thoughts." Autumn hesitated. "I don't think I should, you pissed the department off this time." Maka didn't seem concerned by her statement, she continued to clear a place for Autumn, "They will get over it."

"I don't know. They aren't yet." Autumn sat next to Maka as she showed her the content in the evidence folder.

"What do you make of this?"

Maka handed over the obituary and images of the other evidence they had found.

Autumn looked over them, "You know that the cartel has been more active on the reservation. This would be a clever way to communicate around them and the gangs. Using the internet could be tracked. Did you notice the second obituary?"

Autumn handed the paper back to Maka.

Maka read aloud, "Tom James River leaves behind his family in the HK district. I'm not sure what this means?"

Alan speaks up from the couch, "TJ…. Tijuana, maybe?"

"Yes, and HK, Hong Kong district where nothing good happens."

Autumn looked again at the paper. "There are numbers 011 52 664."

Maka spoke over her. "It's an international phone number."

Alan was curious he hadn't spoken to any other law enforcement agents from the reservation other than Maka. His curiosity got the best of him, and he had to ask Autumn.

"Autumn, what is it like being an officer on the Reservation, do you know if it is much different than that from officers off the Reservation?" Maka looked up at Alan, she did not approve of his question. "Autumn, you don't have to answer."

Autumn looked at Alan, "I don't mind. Well, here we only have about forty-eight officers who serve over 25,000 residents covering 3,500 square miles. There are eight female officers on the force right now. It fluctuates between 32 and 48 depending on if some are sick, on leave, or training, we never know."

"You are so understaffed, I can't imagine." Alan was stunned.

"When I first started in 2004, I felt like I had a child abuse case here and there. Now it's once a week. What needs to stop is the parents, and grandparents need to stop abusing their children, these children end up dying." Autumn stood up and walked toward Alan.

Alan couldn't hold back, "That's something that would rip your heart apart if you ever had to see it."

"You have no idea, children with bruises all over their bodies, bites. And that's something some of the officers see almost weekly. Domestic violence and suicide also make up most of our cases."

"Are there preventative programs in place to help?" Alan asked.

"No, not enough funding."

Maka interrupted, "Autumn, can we step outside."

The women excused themselves and went out the back door.

In the kitchen, the ladies lined up food on the counter for everyone to serve themselves. Annie slowly made her way into the living room and gently sat next to Alan on the sofa. She didn't want to interrupt his typing, so she sat with her hands crossed in her lap, patiently, and just quietly observing everyone in the house. Her skin was slightly weathered, her hair a beautiful white with a hint of pepperish black and gray, tied back with a piece of beaded leather. She wore bright colors of red, white, yellow, and green. She radiated a peaceful presence, patience, and kindness. Her eyes told silent stories only the soul could feel.

Alan watched Annie out of the corner of his eye, he finished typing and gently started to close his laptop.

Annie softly cleared her throat, "You seem to be an important man from California. Why are you traveling across the countryside with our Maka?"

"To help her find the answers she is looking for and to help solve the case of my student." Alan finished closing his laptop and was putting it back in his bag.

"You liked this young man, why?"

"He was bright, talented and he had a story to tell. I wanted to help him. He was one of my most interesting students. There was something special about his perception of the life he lived and the story that burned inside him that he wanted to tell."

"Forgive me, it is not common for a white man to take interest in helping our people."

Alan turned so he could see her better and look her in the eyes.

"I understand, what has happened to your people is inexcusable. I'm here to help."

Annie shifted a bit, so she could lean closer to Alan.

"I know I can see it in your eyes. This young man had a fascination with Wounded Knee. Though sounds like he had gotten tangled up in something he wasn't prepared to fight."

"Annie, what is his sister's name? How well do you know her?"

"Her name is Aiyana. We knew her from the time she was very small. She was shy at times, but always positive, caring, and helpful. Had this dream to bring back the old ways to the reservation. She was sure the highly processed and refined foods of the Western diet were wreaking havoc on our general population. She believed she could return our original diet to heal our people and teach. From what I understand, she and her brother were as close as they could be after he was adopted. Then he left for better education and planned on bringing back what he had learned. I think he wanted to do some kind of movie thing; I don't know much about those things. But Aiyana is an old soul, she would sit and listen to my stories, what seemed like for hours. Sometimes she would take notes." She gave a little laugh.

"Sounds like a lovely young lady. May I ask what happened, why she and Paythan were separated?"

Annie leaned into Alan and placed her hand gently on his forearm.

"Life on the reservation is much different than your California life, young man. Many times, young parents cannot afford their children and are trapped by the dark spirits of alcohol and drugs. We are a spiritual people, drugs are their spirit, and want to take all of our children. It looks like evil looking back at you. The suicide spirit is its brother, and they work together to take our kids. Sometimes the grandparents raise the children, or they are put in foster care. Our people feel hopeless and so they turn to drugs. Then the children suffer from this."

Auntie walked into the room to let them know it was time to eat, "Food's ready, eat while it is still hot." She caught a little bit about what they were speaking about, "What are you two talking about? Seems serious."

"This young man was asking about Aiyana and her brother. You know more about them, tell him."

"What would you like me to tell him?"

Alan decided to interrupt, "I was just asking Annie what Aiyana was like and hoping to learn something about her and Paythan that may help us."

"Out of all their siblings they were the closest, they had dreams. You probably knew this about Paythan."

"Yes, I did. He was a wonderful writer."

"Aiyana wanted to go to California with Paythan after the protest. She wanted to go to school and get a degree so she could come back to the reservation and teach. I would find her with a circle of little kids around her as she told them stories, usually the ones Annie had shared."

Maka and Autumn were talking in the backyard, with a few children that were playing scattered about, giggling as they disappeared around the corner of the house.

"Maka what are you thinking, why are you here?"

Maka was offended "I don't know what you mean. I'm just trying to solve my case."

"It's more than that and you know it. You brought a white man here! You know nothing good will come of this."

"Stop, he has been very helpful."

"Where is your partner?"

"He was re-assigned when I told him we had to work with the reservation. He said they wouldn't collaborate with us."

"He was right." Autumn stopped walking and grabbed Maka by the arm.

"You shouldn't be on the Res. You left, remember."

Maka pulled away from her, "Only to be able to do more."

"You left your people for the Marshals."

"So I could do more for the Res. It is the only way I can see to make a real difference here."

"You look like shit, you look exhausted. When was the last time you slept through a whole night? Are you still working around the clock?"

"I'm making a difference."

"For who?" Autumn asked.

Maka was tormented by her past inactions.

"For the victims, for my sister." Maka walked away from her.

"Maka, you know this is a never-ending war."

"I know. It's big business. Some days it feels impossible with the politics and trying to fight the internet. But when you bring home even one girl and you see the look of relief in her eyes, it makes it all worth it."

"Your sister is not your fault, when are you going to stop punishing yourself?"

"That's your opinion and that is the past. Will you help me now? Help me find Aiyana and bring resolution to Paythan's death. I believe he was murdered trying to find his sister."

Autumn seemed nervous, she kept looking around, "You put me in an awkward position Maka. You know I'm here for you, but you are asking a lot. It could cost us both our careers, maybe our lives."

"I know sister, but I have to try. It has trafficking written all over it! I have to shine a light on this, hold them accountable. It is too hard to ignore the human cost of what we are doing."

She felt increasingly betrayed by the FBI and local law enforcement.

"But how do you expect to do that with a teacher?"

Maka thought about it for a quick moment.

"I know she wouldn't want me to stop. She could have been saved if someone would have seen it through and if people didn't give up so easily. Alan has been a tremendous help. The FBI and ICE pulled agents off the case because of funding and jurisdictional restrictions, limiting us. I had to get creative to pull in as many resources as I could. I didn't see this twist coming."

"You need to reach back out to your agency for some support now with this new discovery in your case. You cannot cross the border without the proper paperwork, even if you do find them how will you get them back without it?"

The back door slammed open against the house; Auntie yelled out "Food is getting cold."

Autumn placed her hand on Maka's shoulder and looked her in the eyes, "And sister, you need to know Chief Hurd sent me here looking for you, his orders were to ensure you left the Reservation."

Auntie waved to the girls, turned, and walked back inside.

Alan was still talking with Annie.

"You must be starving, let's get a plate." Annie slides forward as Alan stood extending his arm to help her up. Maka saw him helping her, she found herself appreciating him even more. Maka leaned forward, her eyes wide open, a little crinkle in her nose. Autumn noticed how she was looking at Alan. Autumn whispered in her ear, "Maka, what do you think you're doing?"

Her question broke Maka's endearing gaze, "I don't know what you mean."

Autumn looked over at Alan helping Annie to the kitchen. Maka didn't know how to respond, nervous, she walked over and picked up her computer and the folders to clear the table while avoiding answering her. Changing the subject, "You know the kids around here, who was Aiyana hanging out with?"

"I know she was spending time with Dakota, Kay, and a couple of boys. They stayed clean, from what I know. We would find them at all the Pow Wow and participating in community stuff. Last I heard a group of them were borrowing the van from the community center and going to the big protest."

"Who are the boys?"

"Chayton was one of them.

"Where do they hang out?"

"I see them around all the usual places mostly."

The tone on Autumn's radio went off, she was getting a call from dispatch. "9-1-8-Sam Officer…"

Autumn turned down the volume.

"I have to go. Bye, everyone."

She raced out the door, everyone could hear her tires spinning and the sound of the siren slowly disappearing as she drove off. As if nothing happened, they gathered around the table to eat, a couple of chairs short Maka and Alan return to the sofa.

"Everything is delicious, thank you." Alan bites into a piece of fry bread.

Maka wondered if he was comfortable. "We need to find Aiyana's friends before we leave tomorrow."

The ladies overheard Maka, one of them spoke out, "You should go to the park tonight, talk to the kids there."

"Do any of you have any pictures of Aiyana and her friends?"

Auntie got up from the table and grabbed her cell phone, scrolling through she walked over to Maka and Alan to show them the images on her phone.

"I only have these from last year's Pow Wow." Pointing out the group of kids in the picture.

"Please send that to me." Maka seemed to have lost her appetite, she placed her plate on the coffee table in front of her, grabbed her phone, and waited for the images to come through.

While she waited for the photos to transfer, she began to pack her things, "Auntie, thank you for dinner. We need to get on the road soon."

Akénuŋpa

12

Moments later, Maka and Alan were driving through the town of Oglala, the sun had disappeared, and a faint glow still illuminated the darkening sky.

"Maka, can I ask you something?"

"Yes."

"Why does there seem to be friction between you and Autumn?"

Maka hesitated for a moment before answering him.

"It's nothing."

Alan sensed she was uncomfortable, but he felt the importance of what was going on.

"If I'm going to help you, shouldn't you be able to trust me enough to tell me what is going on?"

"It was a long time ago when I decided to pursue U.S. Marshal versus staying an officer on the reservation. I felt I could help the reservation if I worked for the government. Growing up, my family…my sister was victimized, lured by a man who forced her into this evil world they have created. She was murdered. I vowed I would honor her and put an end to this evil."

They found themselves deeper into the city Alan couldn't help but compare these streets to Skid Row in Los Angeles, or even a third-world country. As Maka drove slower, Alan could see the signs of poverty and despair were evident, a young girl holding a three-month-old baby only wearing a diaper, a young man smoking a cigarette sitting next to them, trash cluttering what appears to be their front yard. He wondered how the community could rise out of this depression.

They turned a corner getting closer to the park, they saw a lot of commotion and people gathered around. She rolled down her window, she could hear a woman crying, more wailing, "My daughter." She could see two police vehicles parked by the crowd.

She quickly pulled over, looked at Alan. "Do you want to wait here?"

"No, I'll come."

They jumped out of her car and made their way through the people that were gathered around a tree. She looked up and saw a rope dangling from the tree, on the ground was a young girl, who appeared not to be moving.

Autumn was talking to the woman crying, the second officer was tending to the victim's body.

Autumn looked over at Maka and shook her head no. Telling her to stay back.

Maka stopped and waited for Autumn and the officer to take control of the situation. Alan walked up next to Maka.

"What's going on?"

Maka was at first saddened by the initial impact then she shifted to anger. Then she said sarcastically, "Just another day on the res."

"What does that mean?"

She started to walk away from him.

"Another suicide."

Alan stood in awe.

"Wait here for a minute please."

Maka decided she and Alan needed to go find Chayton and Kay. She walked toward Alan.

"Nothing I can do here, let's go."

"Do you know the kids we are looking for?"

"No. Only what they shared back at the house."

"If these girls were trafficked, wouldn't they be taken to Tibet or something?"

Maka looked at Alan in disbelief.

"It's not like the movies, Alan. They are tricked, manipulated, and then threatened." She takes a deep breath and pauses. "The girls and women aren't exposed to many things off the reservation and are a little more gullible, they're young, and naïve, they get taken advantage of. And a lot of the time in trafficking situations it's family members or friends of family. Sometimes their parents sell their children for drugs and money."

"That's awful."

"Have you noticed, talking about trafficking is like a taboo, people avoid it and pretend it's made up? Or worse they say the victims chose this lifestyle. They don't, ya know."

She became discomposed and gathered feelings.

"They are forced into it. And it's not like in the movies, they make them dance at strip clubs, go to big sporting events like Super Bowls, they have underground clubs. A lot of those rappers run those clubs like in Atlantic City. The raw truth, Alan, is it's an evil web, children from six months and into their late teens are sold for sex. Child trafficking is intertwined with high-up criminal activities. It's on the internet. There are people on a very high level making a fortune from child trafficking. It is a multi-billion-dollar industry, more than drugs. This doesn't exist in isolation. It's part of a despicable ecosystem of criminality, the most insidious and evil form of enslavement."

Alan felt embarrassed, "I'm sorry. I have not been exposed to any of this, I must admit it's a bit surreal. He could feel how passionate she was and caring. He didn't know what to say. She was right, it is uncomfortable to talk about, and he didn't know why. It just was.

"I can feel your passion for wanting to fight for these children, it's commendable."

"Don't get me wrong, I'm human, there are days I count down the hours until my shift is over, meanwhile I keep up the façade. In my soul, this is my mission and purpose, Alan. Law enforcement to me is a shield to protect the people from having to see the dark, evil world that we as agents have to see on a daily basis. We live between two worlds every day. One of those worlds most people don't even know exists. And if they do, they close their eyes to it."

Their Jeep came to a rolling halt, the only light coming from street-lights and one working light over the basketball court. The park was filled with older kids playing basketball, some sitting on picnic tables, others tailgating. Most were smoking, drinking out of beer cans, and some of the young women leaning into the arms of young men.

"We're here."

Maka took her phone and checked the photo she had of the young man.

"Maybe you should stay in the car. I'll ask if anyone has seen him."

Alan studied the surroundings; he couldn't help but think to himself he felt he was in an episode of *Dateline*. He shook his head yes. "If you think it's best." He didn't mind staying in the car this time.

"I do. I'll be back." Maka left the Jeep. Alan watched as she became a faint silhouette in the darkness, walking towards some of the kids sitting on an old grey Oldsmobile.

Cautiously approaching several kids gathered around the car, Maka made eye contact with a young male sitting with his girl. He was wearing gang colors and so were the other boys slumping around the car. The group became silent the closer Maka got to them.

"Hey, do you know this guy? His name is Chayton and his girlfriend is Kay?" She showed the picture from her phone.

The young man steps toward to look closely at the phone, taking one last puff from his cigarette before flicking it onto the ground in front of Maka's boot. She never took her eyes off of him or the others.

"What's it to you? Why are you looking for him?" he walked closer to Maka getting in her face. His girl slid off the hood of the car and joined him.

Maka reached in her back pocket for her credentials, "No one is in trouble, I just need to ask him a couple of questions. I'm looking for friends of his, Dakota and Aiyana. Do you know them?" she flashed her badge. The young woman grabbed her boyfriend's arm and pulled him back a few steps.

He threw up his arms and walked back to the car leaning on it, grabbed his beer staring her in the eyes, threw his head back, finished the can, crunched it, and threw it on the ground in between them.

"So, it's like that," shaking her head. "Ya know, this is why our people are in the state they are in, we should be helping each other."

She looked around and decided to try asking some of the others hanging around the court. Now she couldn't see her Jeep and knew Alan would not be able to see her. She walked through the shadows of the park, asking several people and no one said anything, even if they knew something, no one would speak. She crossed over to the basketball court, frustrated, ready to make a statement to interrupt their game. The boys stared for a moment as she kept walking and then began playing again as if she was never there. Out of the shadows from behind a tree, a young woman appeared, startling Maka a bit.

The girl was wearing a revealing tight V-neck t-shirt, torn jeans, and boots. It was one of the girls Maka had seen by the car.

"I know Chayton and Kay. Are they in trouble?" she asked Maka abruptly.

Maka had to take a small step back observing her surroundings. "No. I need their help." The girl was nervous her friends would see her talking to Maka, she stayed out of their line of sight.

"They haven't been out much. They hang out a lot at Kay's house. It's a trailer, off the highway going toward the pipeline camp." She started walking away to get back to her friends. Maka gave her a nod of gratitude "Thank you."

Back at the Jeep, Alan was getting restless. As Maka approached the car, he was getting out.

"Are you ok?" Alan asked in a panicked tone.

"Yes, we have one more stop."

Akéyamni

13

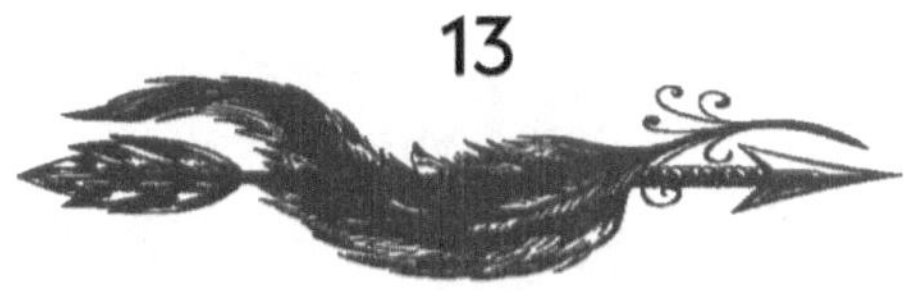

The road was overflowing with darkness, Maka drove cautiously down the desolate road, watching for any movement. Not a flicker of light in sight, only the high beams from her Jeep lit the way. There were no addresses for the homes on the reservation, the only way to find someone's residence was by a landmark and a description of their house, the color of their roof was usually helpful. The description she was given of Kay's house was just on the edge of town, the driveway just past the large boulder, with the red roof. She knew it would be impossible to see the color of the roof at this time of night. Focused intently on her surroundings as she drove, she thought back how frustrating it was back when she was a tribal officer and they would get emergency calls. She recalled how long it took for them to find the house that called for help. The calls were usually domestic violence and sometimes by the time the officers arrived it was too late. She remembered one young mother who called. Her boyfriend lost his job, drank himself into a rage, and took it out on her and the children. Lost in thought Alan snapped her out of it when he saw something on the side of the road up ahead.

"Is that a coyote?" he asked.

Maka slowed down, she stared at what appeared to be a coyote as all they could see was the head at first. Then suddenly she realized it wasn't a coyote.

"Don't make eye contact." She snapped at Alan.

He turned and looked at her, then back out his window.

"I'm serious Alan."

Turning back to her. "Why?"

"It's a skinwalker."

"A what?"

Maka picked up her speed to pass as quickly as she could, not to make any eye contact or even acknowledge they saw it. She knew it was dangerous to speak of the skinwalker, it was believed they were once shamans for their tribes, and in desperate times, to protect their tribes they started to tap into some dark magic. These were usually naked humans that could take the shape of anything, typically an animal. There wasn't much known about them because no one would share skinwalker lore.

"We can't speak of it, it will hear us, they feed off fear."

Alan wasn't sure if she was just playing with him or if she was serious. She seemed very serious and adamant, not giving any energy to whatever, it was they saw. Curious, he decided to google what a skinwalker was as she continued to drive. She looked over at Alan, he had his head down searching for an internet connection.

"I think we are getting closer."

She noticed some large rocks and slowed down looking for a driveway.

Alan was looking intently, trying to help her find the driveway.

"Is that it?"

"Looks like it."

Off in the distance, she saw only the glow of the interior lights of a house that flickered through the windows. She turned onto the driveway, pulling up slowly to the house, casing the area. She came to a stop, put her 9mm in her waistband, and looked at Alan.

"Stay behind me." Alan nodded as they got out of the car.

Cautiously they walked to the front door, it was a double-wide trailer, one of the cleaner ones they had seen all day. The windows were open, and they could hear the television, some light chatter. Walking onto the small single-person porch of five steps leading to the front door, Maka went first, Alan stayed at the bottom. She had to knock twice when she heard scrambling in the house. She stepped to the side trying to catch a glimpse through the window. The door slowly opened, and Kay kept the door between her and Maka.

"What do you want?" Kay abruptly asked as she kept the door cracked just enough to be able to talk.

"Kay?" Maka asked.

"Yes, who are you?" she answered rudely.

Maka repositioned herself. "Can we talk a moment? I'm the agent investigating the death of Paythan and hoping you could help me find his sister."

Kay slammed the door in her face. Maka looked down at Alan, he didn't know how to react. She was going to knock on the door again, maybe bang on it this time, as she raised her hand to do so, the door opened widely.

"Can we come in? Is Chayton here?" Maka started to advance forward. Kay stepped aside and allowed her to enter, Alan right on her heels.

"Chayton" Kay called out. A young man, hair pulled back in a ponytail, wearing a t-shirt and jeans with tennis shoes covered in dried mud, his hands pushed deep into his pockets appeared from the hallway shadows.

Alan observed old worn furniture scattered throughout, old magazines and papers spread out on an old coffee table, pizza boxes on the end table, the couch a red/orange color, and threads hanging out of the arm of the chair.

"When was the last time you saw Paythan and his sister?" Maka asked quickly.

Chayton looked at Kay, they looked scared and hesitated for a moment. "Last was the night after the protest. I drove Paythan back to the gas station to pick up Aiyana and Dakota, but they were gone. They left in a black SUV with dark tinted windows." He looked at Kay for support.

"We got chased off by the fucking skinheads and had to leave them. But we came right back about a half hour or so later. You know how the assholes get."

"What happened when you went back?"

"Paythan and I looked all over for them, they weren't there. He made me take him back to the hotel to get his bike. He rode off that night."

He took a deep breath and looked at Maka. Kay, nudged him, "Tell her."

"Fine. Paythan asked us to help him find her, he got Mato to let us use his horses and we all rode along the river to that hotel. He got a tip from someone that they saw a black SUV with blacked-out windows go down that road. The road that leads to that old motel."

"Did he say anything more about who was driving the SUV?"

"No. He never said."

Chayton lit a cigarette.

"It's the one back by the Tongue River. You can't get through without four-wheel drive."

Maka thought for a moment, this she agreed. If she hadn't had her Jeep, it would have not been possible for her and Alan to get back there.

"Then what happened?" Maka asked.

"Paythan had us doing old warrior tradition kind of stuff. He said it was our duty as the men to protect our family 'wicasa was'aka,'" he said," means strong men."

"We followed the river. He had us do a prayer ceremony, some old guy… Bear something was his name. He came up and did it with us, he was kind of cool and told us stories around the campfire."

"Blue Bear?" Maka interrupted.

"Ya, that's it. He was alright." Chayton started to pace the room a bit. He went on to say "Later, like the next night, we went up the river. Got to that hotel. We stayed by the river and watched. Saw some men off in the distance, looked like a party or something. Then two big black SUVs came back there, Mato and the other guys got spooked and took off. Paythan and I stayed for a bit and watched them go inside, it was getting cold, and we didn't see anything I thought was weird. Sun started coming up and I convinced him to come back with me. We like rode back and then he told me to go ahead and turned around. He told me something didn't feel right, and he wanted to check something. He was sure he was going to find them. That was the last I saw him. Mato's horse found its way back and we tried to find Paythan, but he wasn't answering our calls or anything. I told officer "Chaska," and she said they would take it from there and we needed to leave it alone."

He put out his cigarette and lit another.

"Is it true, is he dead?"

Maka responded while looking around the room. "Yes, he is. Did you tell Chaska what you saw at the hotel?"

"No way, man. He loved his sister; they had big plans to do some stuff. Better than being trapped here."

"What else can you tell me about that night after the protest?"

Chayton thought about it for a bit, Kay blocked Maka from walking past her. Maka turned and walked back towards the door.

"Anything you can tell me could be helpful."

Alan stayed close to the door observing, listening.

Kay spoke up, "That's about it. We went to the protest and when they broke it up, we stopped at the station for gas. Aiyana and Dakota were inside getting snacks when we got chased off by the skinheads. I texted Aiyana to stay inside and we would be back to get them."

"Did she text you back?" Alan interrupted.

Everyone in the room was so silent they could hear frogs' singing echoing in the night, Maka stepped closer to him.

"Yes, she just said "Okay. They were scared hurry back, kinda thing."

"Do you still have the text and her cell number?" Maka asked.

Kay took her phone from her back pocket and scrolled through "Yes, I still have it." She found it and showed it to Maka.

Maka took the phone and took a picture of the text and Aiyana's phone number.

"Did you hear from her anymore after that?"

Chayton looked at Kay and shook his head to say no. Kay looked at Maka and Alan, hesitating, "No."

Maka didn't believe her and decided to press. "Are you sure, she is supposed to be your best friend? If you know anything don't hold it back, her life could be depending on it."

Kay looked at Chayton again, the look on his face seemed to make her very uncomfortable.

Maka looked at Alan. "Let's go. They clearly don't care about their friends."

Alan opened the door for them to leave, Maka followed him out.

"Wait!" Kay stepped closer to Maka. "Chayton, they should know."

Maka stopped and turned, "Know what?"

"I got a weird message from Aiyana on Instagram, it was just okiya she doesn't usually speak our native language when we message and there were no more messages after that. We didn't know what to do."

"Can you show me?" Maka followed Kay, she picked up her phone and showed Maka.

"She messaged help. Why didn't you call the police?"

Frustrated, Maka held onto Kay's phone. "I need to make a call, you wait here." Alan stood in the doorway observing.

Stepping outside away from the house Maka made a call to a fellow agent she knew she could trust. She was the forensic examiner for the federal unit they were assigned to.

"Barton, I need you to trace this number."

A bit of time had passed, and Maka came back inside, "Thank you." She walked to the door and hesitated, Alan wasn't sure what she was going to do. Maka pulled a business card from her back pocket. "If you think of anything, anything that might help us in finding her, call me." She handed the card and phone to Kay, and looked at Alan, allowing him to walk out the door first. It was as if they had telepathy and knew what the other was thinking.

Back in the car, they drove through the night to Rapid City.

"Did you get the information you needed from them?" Alan asked softly.

"I hope so, I'm having the IP traced from the message sent. If my intuition is right, it will confirm where the girls might be."

"You can trace a location just from that?"

"Hopefully, it's a process they will go through using the Stingray. It collects information from mobile phones and computers, it can track users. It will take some time and if it is used again, it will help us tremendously in narrowing down, if not pinpointing her location."

She had a wealth of resources at her disposal—top-secret databases, surveillance tools, and equipment not made known to the general public. Surveillance teams monitored phone calls, read through emails, and could trace them.

"Big brother is always watching, as they say," Alan commented.

"It has saved countless lives and might help us save these girls."

"I'm sure controversial."

"Most things are these days."

Akétopa

14

The sound of jet engines vibrated through the cabin of the Boeing 757. Alan looked out the small window, the city of San Diego looked peaceful from that perspective. He noticed the sequence of flashing lights outlining the edge of the runway as they approached. He had a few more minutes to finish working on his screenplay before they landed.

Wheels down, he looked over at Maka, she had put on her glasses while working on her computer, filing the paperwork they were going to need to get the girls back to the United States. He caught himself starting to grin as he got lost in appreciating her dedication to her work, thinking to himself that she looked awfully cute with her glasses on. He couldn't help himself; he couldn't take his eyes off her, his heart beat a little faster and everything around them ceased to exist. Suddenly, the skipping and hard bounce from the plane's wheels hitting the runway jarred them both. Some of the files fell to the floor, and they both quickly bent over to collect them. Nearly bumping heads, Alan still couldn't take his eyes off her. As they rose in sync Alan leaned in gently kissing her on the lips. She reciprocated, and they held their lips together sharing a deep breath that suddenly seemed one. His lips resting against hers, Alan softly ran the back of his index finger along her cheek, then jawline, and using his thumb outlined her lower lip. One last inhale between them, and as they exhaled slowly their lips tenderly began to separate. His hand slowly caressed her neck and then held her hand, giving it a gentle squeeze. They didn't lose eye contact, sharing an alluring smile.

Alan checked his messages while he waited for Maka to finish checking out the rental car. He had a message from Jerry. He thought he better call him back, he stepped away to a little bit of a quieter area to make the call.

Jerry picked up so quickly that Alan didn't even hear it ring, "Jer?'

"Alan where the hell are you? The heads are breathing down my neck! What the hell man!"

"Just stop for a second. I still have close to two weeks before the deadline."

"They don't give a shit; you know they want to see some pages! Why won't you tell me where you are?"

Alan began pacing back and forth, keeping an eye on Maka. "Well, don't be mad, I'm in San Diego heading to Tijuana."

"What the hell! *Why?* Don't give me some bullshit about Betty Hutton being part Mexican now!"

Alan tried to explain but Jerry kept cutting him off. "The trail for Paythan's death led us down here. I need to finish this, Jer."

"Alan, you need to get your ass back to the studio and finish this script. They are going to fire you!"

"Cover for me just a couple more days. I will send you some pages."

"I don't know what more I can do; I have been covering for you for almost two weeks."

"If you don't hear from me in two days, call me, and if I don't answer send help."

When I get back you need to help me pitch this story about Paythan, this is a big screen story!"

Maka finished with the paperwork and motioned to Alan to go. He was still pacing and talking on the phone. She walked toward him, "Jer, I have to go, I will have it done. Talk to you in a couple of days!"

"Alan, don't you hang up on me."

"Bye, Jer"

"I'm sorry, didn't mean to interrupt. Is everything OK?"

"No. We need to stop so I can send some pages to the producer. I didn't expect to be gone as long as we have been, let alone going to Tijuana."

After picking up a rental car they began traveling on the highway in a Honda Accord. Alan shifted around in his seat, "Couldn't we have gotten something with a little more legroom?"

Maka found humor in that he looked like a little boy fidgeting in his seat. "We don't want to stand out too much in Tijuana." She replied.

"We are almost to the border."

"How long does it take to process the paperwork you submitted?"

"Shouldn't take longer than 24 hours for this, hopefully, sooner."

As they approached the border crossing, Maka looked Alan in the eyes and said, "I will do the talking," she was very stern. She didn't want to raise any red flags.

The car rolled slowly through the lane, the border patrol agent, female, Latino, petite, but gave off the energy of being in her power; "passport."

Maka handed their enhanced drivers' licenses to the agent. "Citizenship?" The agent inspected the exterior of the vehicle "How many are in the vehicle?"

"From the U.S. Just the two of us," Maka answered. Alan was still fumbling with his phone. The agent looked at him, "Where are you going?" The agent was still holding their credentials.

"Just to the beach for a couple of days, to relax." Maka smiles. The agent handed back their licenses and nods them to move forward.

Alan started the navigation on his phone. Maka drove through the bumper-to-bumper traffic, they got stopped at a red light, a man stepped in front of traffic and tried to wash the windows on the cars. On the other side of the street a young girl, maybe thirteen years old, runs out with an even younger girl, maybe seven years old. The older girl got on her knees and the young girl jumped on her shoulders. They did a dance and the younger girl started to juggle. Seconds before the light turned green the little girl jumped down and ran up to the windows of cars with a hat for tips. Alan sat in awe watching the people selling food, souvenirs, and even stray dogs wandering in between cars looking for a handout as well.

"I was thinking, I can make a couple calls to some friends who work for the papers, USA Today or CNN. Maybe they could put out a story, and share the girls' pictures?"

"No. This can't leak out. We need to build a case that would not only prove our charges but also deflate their defenses."

"I don't understand."

"Have to remember that this is an ongoing, underground, and brutal exploitation of children, women, and men. There are much higher powers that are behind much of this. We have to be careful."

Maka pulled out her firearm and placed it on her lap. "Alan, can you reach my bag?" He reached behind and put it in his lap. "Open it please, on the bottom, do you see that leather case, grab it." Alan put the small leather case on his lap and put her bag on the back seat. "Open the case." He unzipped the case, it flapped open revealing a Glock Gen5 9mm, clip on the side. "You can put the bag back. Thanks."

Alan looked at Maka. "I want you to put the clip in it. You are going to carry it." Alan unsure, his forehead started to bead with sweat, "Maka, I haven't shot a gun in probably twenty years—on a hunting trip and I missed the deer."

Maka put her hand on his knee, "You won't need it, please just carry it." His hands trembled, palms sweating, he tried to put the clip in but he had it backward. Maka tried to weave through traffic, then noticed him struggling, "Just flip it over and it will slide right in."

Alan stopped for a moment and raised his eyebrows.

Maka saw the look on his face and thought, *Oh geez, men.*

He did as she instructed and secured the clip, slid the leather case under his seat, and the gun dropped on the floor landing next to his feet. He practically jumped out of his seat, leaned down, and gently picked it up, Maka ran her hand over the back of his head, gently caressing down the back of his neck. They looked into each other's eyes, he tried to smile back at her but he was too nervous.

The streets were crowded as they drove in, "Zona Norte, it's known as the red light district." They passed vivid urban art.

"Also, known to be the biggest trafficking area. Most of the clubs are fronts for brothels, so if my intuition is right then they brought the girls down here from the Res," Maka explained.

Driving slowly through the city, club after club, certain parts looked as if they were the aftermath of war. There were people, families, and children living amongst it all.

Maka turned down a street, dark with just as much traffic, on one side was a river. She pointed out, "I think that is where they found Paythan, down by the river. This is supposed to be the most dangerous road in Tijuana."

As she drove, they could see shadowy figures crouched along the highway meridian, it appeared they were openly cooking and shooting heroin. Alan was speechless, he reflected keeping his thoughts to himself, about the reservation as it was just hundreds of miles north of here and yet these two places almost mirrored one another. Two very separate worlds, both seem to have a common thread in them, the humans that shared a world that had exiled and demoralized them. Their existence didn't seem to have much meaning to them. Many of them suffered from addiction and many had given up. What was astonishing was there was another world in between that seemed to conveniently have its blinders on, going on the day to day, as if these communities didn't exist or need help. Much like the Res, the people in TJ seemed to have had their humanity taken away from them.

Moments later, pulling up alongside the road, the river just steps away, Maka hesitated, assessing the area, only to see dark silhouettes moving through the darkness.

"Is this safe?" Alan observed the area looking out his window.

"Not at all," Maka answered, putting her gun in front of her waistband, and pulling her shirt over it. She reached into the back seat, finding her hoodie. As she pulled it over her head, "You stay here, I'm going to see if I can find out if anyone will talk to me. Do not leave this vehicle." Maka looked him sternly in the eye. "I'm serious Alan. Don't."

Alan was concerned, "I understand," he grabbed her hand, "but if you are not back in ten minutes, I'm coming to look for you."

Maka cautiously walked toward the river. Even though San Diego was about ten miles north, the sky was thick with clouds of pollution. There was an overwhelming pungent smell of sewage coming from the river, no moon, no stars that she could see, and death lingered in the air. She began reflecting on all the information she had been studying, recalling the pictures of where they found Paythan's bike. She whispered to her ancestors to help guide her, speaking her prayers. She knew she needed to trust and follow that gnawing intuition in her spirit that was leading her, it had never failed her before.

The darkness of night lay heavy as she walked ahead, the only light that could be found was the glow from a few scattered fire pits along the river. Her eyes adjusted, revealing the path, she could feel the energy of the depressed people that surrounded her. She couldn't understand why Paythan would come here of his own will.

Once she reached the edge of the river, she found the spot where Paythan's bike was discovered. Lowering to her knees she felt the wet, moss-covered ground and whispered, "Paythan, talk to me, what were you doing around here?" She took a moment of silence, absorbing the surroundings, then pulled up some of the pictures taken around the site the day Paythan's body was found.

She began to feel a presence, as if being stalked. Slowly turning left, then right, and looking behind her she caught the movement of at least two bodies disappearing behind a tree and some bushes. Placing her right hand on the butt of her gun, her finger rested on the trigger and her thumb was ready to relieve the safety.

She could feel eyes on her, "Hola te veo. Salga." Maka yelled out to her stalkers to come out. A rustle came from the branches. She slid her gun from her waistband down around her right side, trying to conceal it and not alarm anyone prematurely.

"Salga. Come out now," she said with more authority. A man came from the umbra slowly, as he came closer Maka felt uneasy and yelled out "Close enough." He wasn't stopping. "Suficientemente cerca!" she tried in Spanish. He continued.

"Speak English?" she yelled. Still silent, she clicked the safety off her gun. He stopped only four feet in front of her, she could barely see the whites in his eyes, they were almost completely black, his hands in his back pockets he just stared at her. She stared back, suddenly feeling her heart start to the race, then began to pound as if it were going to come out of her chest. Still no words, she felt paralyzed, as if he had looked through her eyes into her soul trying to penetrate hers with his darkness. She found herself saying prayers to her ancestors to protect her from this evil presence.

The man said nothing, not being able to take the silence Maka spoke out, "What do you want!" Still no response, the man just cocked his head to the side and continued to stare into her eyes. She felt as if he had reached into her chest and was squeezing, crushing her heart. She raised her firearm and said "Wočhékiye kuseyaon miye pheta" a prayer to her ancestors for protection from evil, the man didn't flinch, and he replied "Aho" which meant "thank you." A second man appeared next to the first man, Maka placed both hands around her gun.

"You don't belong here," the second man said in very broken English, "leave now."

Maka kept her gun pointed at the men, feeling the darkness of energy spewing from them. She backed away slowly in the direction of her car, keeping an eye on both men she lowered her gun and began walking quickly, keeping her eye on them and her surroundings until they blurred into the night's darkness.

She rushed back into the car; Alan was taken by surprise. "That didn't go as I planned." Her breath was rapid, hands a little shaken.

Alan was concerned "Are you ok? What happened?"

"Yes, but we aren't going to get any answers here." She reached into her bag that was in the back seat. Alan placed his hand above her knee to comfort her.

"We need to go here" she pulled out a paper that had the name of a club not far from there.

"Are you sure we should continue on tonight?"

"We have to if we have any chance to find Aiyana. At the river, I could feel Paythan. Like he was trying to tell me something. I know she is here; I can feel it."

She looked deeply into Alan's eyes. "I have to try."

Alan leaned over and kissed her on the forehead and said, "I understand, tell me what I can do."

Handing the paper to Alan, "Tell me how to get here."

She started the car and began to drive. Alan found the address on his phone and turned on the volume so Maka could hear the directions.

Maka kept looking in her rear-view mirror, still feeling the heaviness from the dark energy at the river and disappointed that she didn't find more answers there.

The car was filled with a deafening silence, Maka's frustration grew into anger, and she started pounding on the steering wheel "Ugh!" She hit it repeatedly. Alan wasn't sure what he should do, he just let her get it out.

"I'm sorry Alan."

"Please don't apologize, I'm feeling it too."

Moments later they arrived on a street packed with rows of rowdy bars, nightclubs, strip clubs, and prostitution. People crowded the sidewalks as they arrived at the infamous Zona Norte, the red-light district or "Hell." Brothels, massage spas, and hotels offered services to their clients there for sexual tourism.

Both were in awe of what they were witnessing. Alan couldn't help himself blurting out, "I never imagined this."

"People come from all around the country to Tijuana searching for sex. Not only Tijuana, but Atlanta and several other cities around the country. They don't like to talk about it. Been a rise in the kidnapping and recruitment of girls and boys forcing them into it. Haven't you heard of the case of the man from the Midwest who came here to buy baby girls to molest them?"

There were clubs for another block, people lingering, the girls of Coahuila, Paraditas walking the streets, some lined the buildings, and others in the alley hidden in the darkness. They waited for a male shopper. The area was also popular for people who weren't looking for sex, with a bunch of taco stands and shops. What she didn't share with Alan was some of the reasoning why these men came to Tijuana. How these men said things like, "It's too risky to deal with women in the states. They have made it hostile toward men who only want intimacy."

She didn't share that Tijuana was a fantasy land for males.

"This is horrible." Alan found himself experiencing a story, not even his imagination could find the words to write.

Maka slowed down, searching for a club that matched the partial name she found. "There it is." She pointed to the club as they slowly passed by the marque lit bright above the door, a crowd of people walking past. She reached a stop sign at the end of the street. The lights didn't reach this far and darkness overtook the area. Maka pulled over in one of the darkest places she could find.

"This is what we need to do, we are going to take advantage of the tourism. You are going to walk over to that club, and while you are standing there you will be approached by more than one person making you offers of drugs and girls." Alan interrupted her, "Even with the police officers over there?"

"Everyone is involved here; the police turn a blind eye to money. They abuse the girls as well."

Maka's energy went from being a sweet gentle woman to almost rigid, taking all the emotion out of her plan. She was adamant, strong and firm. She expected that the operation they were about to embark on was serious, knowing that Alan was not trained for any of what she was asking of him. From what she knew of him, he had never been exposed to any circumstances like this. She could only pray he wouldn't shut down or fumble, giving them away. She knew what the risks and rewards were, and that he was unaware.

She reached into the back seat and brought up her duffle bag. "Alan, can you do this? I can't go in as you can. Aiyana, Paythan, they are counting on you."

Alan looked behind them and thought about it for a bit, "I don't know if I can pull this off, I have never done anything like this."

"I'll walk you through it, just do as I say, and I will do the rest." Alan nodded his head.

Maka continued to fumble through her bag pulling out clothes. "I will need to change my clothes."

Alan went to reach for his bag, "What should I wear?"

"What you're wearing is great. You are the stereotypical-looking client they are in search of, you look like an LA tourist."

"And that's a good thing?'

"It is tonight. You will walk to the club and unless someone offers you an 'exotic experience' you turn them down. When you get to the club you tell them you are looking for an exotic experience. You have to say it like that, OK?"

"Why?"

"Because then they will give you the options of Native, Latino or Asian girls. We don't have a lot of time for me to explain it all right now."

"Where will you be?"

"Not far behind you. Never make eye contact with me if you see me. Once they take you inside there should be a back room, a secret room, only for clients and you need to play along. Take another look at Aiyana and Dakota's pictures. I won't be able to go in the back with you."

Maka called Alan on his phone, he looked at it as it was ringing, she leaned over and answered it.

"Leave it on, I will be able to hear everything and if you need me just say 'I need you' but keep it in your pocket so they don't take it from you."

Alan started to feel beads of perspiration form on his forehead, and Maka noticed it as well.

"What if they are there? What do I do?"

"Keep calm, tell them that's the girl you want. Then I'll know you found her. They will take you to her. Don't tell her who you are, just talk with her, makeup that you are nervous and want to talk first. Tell her it's your first time, stall as long as you can."

Alan had to wipe his forehead, "It won't be a lie, I'm nervous and it is my first time. What if I get a different girl?"

"Try telling them that you're not interested until you think they showed you all of them. Most of these undergrounds have what they call a 'menu' for the men to choose from, then they take you to a small room, like a stall and the girl is waiting in there. If we are lucky, they will have a menu and you can choose Native girl."

"A menu! This gets sicker by the minute, Maka. I don't know if I can do this."

"Tell them you want a 'date' then tell them half and half."

"Do I want to know what that means?"

"Probably not. You're not going to do any of it, just try and find the girls."

"These people are going to see right through me."

"Alan, you have to try, they get newbies all the time."

Maka leaned in and they hugged, she kissed him a deep kiss, he could feel their connection once again.

It helped him to muster up the courage to walk into the brothel.

"I need to change. You start heading for that club with the blue fox on the window, I'll be a few minutes behind. You can do this; I know you can. Oh, and watch out for the barracudas."

Alan placed his hand on the door, took a deep breath, and opened it. "Barracudas?"

The pit in his stomach was growing to nausea, he felt like he was going to vomit. He didn't want to tell Maka, he got out taking one last look at her, she was already starting to undress. He closed the door and walked towards the brothel.

As she was changing, her phone alerted her that she had a message. She looked, it was the report from the forensic agent, and it showed her the exact location where they could find the last message Aiyana sent. It was from the area of the hotel on the reservation.

***

Alan walked into the lighted streets. *I was right*, he thought to himself. The streets were plagued, there were like cockroaches scattering as he passed. He felt he stood out amongst the crowd, he looked like a tourist, but this was no Disneyland. He thought, *If there is a hell, I'm in it.* It was clear the real parasites were not insects or rodents; it was the human species. The environment, communities, anything living that didn't bring money, fame or power was destroyed, used, or abused. It was the human species that was destroying itself and the planet. His mind raced, causing his heart to race faster, the streets began to swirl.

Still about a block away from the club with the blue fox in the window, he passed several aging buildings housing clubs, brothels, and even what they considered a hotel. As he passed one of the clubs he looked in as the door was wide open. He could see there was a stage with naked women dancing, he watched as the men, clearly Caucasian men, groped at the women, acting like animals, treating the women as if they were prey, as if they were soulless objects only there for the men to abuse them, taunt them, and have their way with them. It disgusted him, he could hardly control the emotions that were welling up inside him as he watched how vile these men were.

As he walked, the sidewalk became denser with a diverse group of people. He passed several young girls leaning against the weathered old buildings, he tried not to make eye contact. Some were flaunting themselves at him, selling themselves, while others looked withdrawn, scared, and didn't acknowledge him. He wondered, what these girls were thinking, what was their story. *How does a girl end up standing on the sidewalk, selling their body as if it was an inanimate object, for men to do as they want, with no regard for their soul?* He couldn't even imagine. One girl, in particular, did catch his eye, she looked like she couldn't be older than thirteen. She was watching the other girls around her, there were a couple of women near them, maybe in their late twenties or early thirties. It appeared as if they were teaching them how to stand and walk. How to work the men walking past. Right shoulder leaned casually against the wall. Chest pushed forward as their left hands rested on their hips which were cocked upward, emphasizing their assets.

One of the women said, "Hey man, you like her. You take her." She pointed to the young girl; the girl looked scared like she wanted to run but there was nowhere for her to go. Alan shook his head no. He tried to continue to walk but was slowed down by a group of people. He could see the club Maka told him to go to not far up.

A local man approached him from behind, startling Alan. "Hola. Go in, you want to watch."

"No. No." Alan started to walk faster; the man followed.

"You want to smoke?" he tried to hand Alan a small bag of marijuana.

"No."

"Girls?"

Alan almost forgot what Maka told him to say. He paused looking around.

"Yes. Exotic. Over there." Alan pointed at the blue fox sign.

"Si. Come with me."

Alan followed the man to the entrance, there was a bouncer guarding the door. The man didn't have to say anything, he walked past the bouncer with a nod, turned to Alan, and pointed where they were going.

The club was dark, with lights that only revealed the dancers, some in cages and others on stage. They were young. Alan couldn't help but stop in shock seeing a young girl in a cage, naked, her round ample cheeks red, her eyes lifeless, her body still not matured. The men clapped, laughing, and yelling vulgar things at the girls. He noticed a heavy-set man near the edge of the stage. There were four girls, one on each side of the stage and one in the middle, dancing, flittering with the men, teasing them for their money. The heavy-set man had a skinny cigar and money in his left hand, he was saying things to the girl that was closest to him. Alan could see she was ignoring him; she was doing her job. The man seemed to be getting frustrated with her ignoring him, he kept looking at the other men standing near him, throwing his hand in the air and complaining. Alan paused to watch while his tour guide was talking with someone by the bar. The heavy-set man pushed another man who was standing too close. The other man shook it off and walked away as the heavy-set man leaned onto the stage and rubbed the leg of the dancer as she passed by him. Alan noticed he didn't seem satisfied when the young girl stopped to dance for some other men. She was out of his reach. The man made his way closer to her, waiving his money. Alan caught her roll her eyes and look over at the bouncer. She danced her way back to take his money, the man teased her and coerced her to get closer, he ran his hand up her inner thigh, cupping in between her legs, grabbing hard. Alan found himself feeling more and more enraged, he started to walk towards the stage when two very large bouncers pushed past and grabbed the heavy-set man, dragging him out of the club. The man was yelling "What the fuck! I spend a lot of money in this place, which is what these girls are here for, that is all they're good for! Get the fuck off me!"

Looking around Alan observed the faces of the girls, their eyes slowly surveying the room, faces masked with indifference and feigned desire.

Alan leaned hard up against the bar; he was scared. Ordering a drink, he noticed a man walking over towards him, leaving a table of about five Caucasian men. The man excused himself to squeeze in between Alan and other people gathered around the bar.

"Mind if I order a drink?"

"No, not at all." Alan moved over as much as he could, but he needed to feel the security of leaning on the bar, his knees were shaking so much he was afraid they would give out and he would fall.

The man got a straight-up tequila, sipping on it, he turned to look at the dancers and struck up a conversation with Alan.

"Reddit?"

"Excuse me?"

"Did you find this place on Reddit?"

"Oh no. A friend recommended it."

"I've been coming here for almost a year after my divorce. I can't find it in California."

Alan thought, OK, I'll bite. "What's that?"

The man continued to say "Intimacy, we just want intimacy with a girl. Right? I mean, I'm not getting laid in the States. But here, all these beautiful women and they do whatever you tell them."

The man put his hand on Alan's shoulder and squeezed it as if he was one of his best buddies.

"I mean where else can you pick and choose from hundreds of beautiful girls to have sex with…right?"

Alan just stared at him in disbelief, he couldn't believe what he was hearing.

"My buddies and I are like fuck this shit, take me to TJ!"

"Pardon my ignorance, but this is how you define intimacy?"

The man took a big sip of his drink and looked at Alan with a blank face. For Alan, it felt as if time stopped, and he was in a different dimension. The man laughed at Alan.

"You're a funny guy."

The man went back to his friends, laughing and dancing while he made his way to the table. Alan turned his back to them and slammed his drink, thinking to himself, *What the hell am I doing here?*

Alan's tour guide came up behind him and tapped him on the arm to follow. As he led Alan to the back corner past the bar, there was a door, covered in black padded leather. Alan was observing the people as they passed by and saw Maka, a version of her he had not seen yet. She was dressed in a very short, sleeveless, black jersey dress. He noticed how revealing the front was immediately and when she turned, he did a double take as it was backless, the seam just resting on the top of her very firm, round buttocks. Her heels were close to six inches high, and the black straps wrapped around her ankle made it look as if there was no end to her legs. She looked at the bartender waiting for her drink, as Alan passed a man next to her tried to talk with her.

Alan saw her flip her hair back as she spoke to the men. He stumbled in jealousy, it took everything in him not to walk over there, he suddenly found himself feeling like a high school boy in love for the first time. All he could think was how he wanted to knock that guy unconscious who was hitting on his girl.

The tour guide pushed the padded door open and let Alan in first. As he slipped into the back room, he looked over his shoulder one last time at Maka. She was holding a short glass that looked like vodka, talking with two men. What he didn't know was that the whole time she was keeping her eye on him. The heavy door closed slowly behind them, and it disappeared into the wall once it shut. There was no sign of a door handle, he couldn't find the door again if he wanted to. There were a few stairs to walk down. It felt like a tunnel, with rounded turns going down. It was quiet, too quiet. Alan realized they were in a soundproof area.

Once they reached the bottom of the stairs, a large, overweight dark-skinned man stood against the wall. Alan looked him over twice, the man's biceps were bigger than any man he had ever seen, including the Hulk. He had to be 6 foot 7 and the muscles rippled across his body; Alan noticed he was carrying a Glock on his waist. His tour guide saw his reaction and said, "Clock-watcher."

The further they walked the more Alan couldn't believe what he was seeing, there was no dignity in this place. They passed several small booths that looked much like voting booths, a couple had a single stool in them, some were empty, and one had a cot. There was no privacy, only a couple had a curtain to cover the door. As they got deeper, they passed booths that were occupied, Alan couldn't bear to look. The smell began to grow stronger the further they went, it was foul, a mixture of cheap perfume, body odor, and a nasty musty smell of sex permeated the room. The sounds were already beginning to echo, and he knew he would never be able to forget.

The man motioned to Alan, "Stop here."

They stopped in front of a curtain, he opened it, and a young Asian girl was sitting on the stool, topless, wearing only a thong. She appeared cold, and her eyes were lifeless. She just stared, emotionless. Alan didn't know what to say or do, he knew it wasn't Aiyana. The man nudged him to go inside, Alan pushed back "No, I said exotic."

"She is. You don't like?"

"No. Native girl." That's all that Alan could seem to get to come out. He was starting to tremble with emotions, fighting the urge to want to save this young girl.

"You said you wanted a date? Come with me."

The man shook his head in frustration. "It will cost you more."

"Fine." Alan followed behind him. They passed a couple more booths, he heard a girl crying, then a slap, and then another. He paused and listened for a moment.

"Stop crying," came from a male voice.

"I don't want to do this," the girl sobbed, "I don't want to be here."

"Yes, you do, or you wouldn't be here," the man responded.

He hesitated to take steps toward the booth, wanting to go and rescue the girl.

"Señor, come with me." The man was firm with Alan, he made him continue.

"Take you to the VIP room, I think you will like that more."

"Si," Alan agreed.

The man did something on his phone, Alan couldn't see what exactly he did. It appeared as if he was messaging someone. They went back and forth for a brief moment.

He could feel the vibration from the music as they got closer to a door. Once inside he found there were private rooms with doors.

After looking at his phone the man pointed "That one."

Alan, uncertain, approached slowly, "This one?"

"Si, go in. You have fifteen minutes." He yelled to the girl inside "half and half" and walked away.

Alan slowly opened the door, a young woman sat on a cot with her back toward them. He couldn't see her face, she had long black hair, it was dirty, oily, and ratted in the back. She sat almost lifeless. He turned and the man waved him inside.

Alan closed the door behind him, "Hello" he whispered. The girl made no effort to look at him. She was in a bra and thong, her skin had chill bumps from head to toe. He tried to talk to her again. "Hello. What's your name?"

Still no response. He stood in silence unsure of what to do, she wasn't moving or talking. Alan couldn't help to wonder if she was on drugs.

"Hi. I'm Alan. What's your name?"

The girl turned a bit, enough for Alan to see her face, "Does it matter?" she replied.

"Yes, it does."

"Where's your hat?"

She looked at him, he now knew this was not the girl they were looking for, but she was Native, and it seemed like she might want help. She looked him up and down, silent, motionless. He had to think quickly as to what to do, he looked at his watch. They both stood in silence, neither moving.

"My hat?"

"Condom."

"Excuse me a moment, I just need to check something." Alan took out his phone he checked his text messages. There was nothing from Maka, he noticed he didn't have cell service.

The young girl spoke, "It won't work in here."

"Oh, oh, thanks. I would like to talk."

"That's how you want to spend what's left of your 15 minutes?"

"Yes, is that ok?"

"Sure, if you don't tell Daddy. He will beat us if we don't perform."

"No one needs to know."

The girl was shivering, she sat on the edge of the bed. She seemed like she might be on something. Alan wished he had a coat to give her, she looked so frail and so young.

"How old are you?"

She hesitated, "15."

"What's your name?"

"Taara."

"Beautiful name." Alan kept looking at this watch, the time seemed to drag. He wasn't sure what was racing faster, his mind or his heart.

Akézaptaŋ

15

Back in the club, Maka was making new acquaintances. She was able to catch the attention of the Daddy who was trying to sway her to join him in his private booth. Maka immediately caught that he was a Romeo Pimp, and he was laying it on thick.

A man in a button-down pressed shirt, nice black slacks, and Italian leather shoes bought Maka another cocktail. "What are you drinking?"

Maka shook her glass, the ice rattled against the side as it only had one sip left. She drank it and said, "Vodka with lime."

The Daddy motioned to the bartender for another drink. "Now you can come join my party. You will fit right in. He handed her the fresh drink and grabbed her hand, guiding her to his booth.

The intense music and the flashing lights created a tripping effect, especially for those high on hallucinogens. Approaching the booth, he introduced Maka to the group.

"Hey, this is…oh, sorry beautiful didn't get your name."

She looked at him and said "Maka. I didn't catch yours?"

"Call me T."

"What does 'T' stand for?"

One of the men sitting in front of them yelled out, "Trouble!"

They all started to laugh.

"No really, Thomas."

Maka pretended to take a small sip of her drink, thinking to herself, *Such a normal name for such an evil monster.* 'T' slapped the guys to move over and make room for them. He was trying hard to persuade her to join them.

"Why are you here, Maka?"

"Looking for a good time, seemed to have made a wrong turn and ended up here."

"Seems like the right turn for me." T placed his hand on her knee sliding it up her thigh and stopping at the edge of her dress. She was relieved when he stopped there.

"We both know why I'm here T. I need money and fast. I stay an independent."

"A lot of demands from a woman who needs money fast."

A slightly older woman approaches T, "I'm ready for you." Maka quickly surmised this woman was the Madam.

"I would like you to show Maka to the back room and get her set up.

Maka stood, put her glass down on the table in front of them. She looked at T as she walked off, always observing everyone and everything around.

The madam took Maka to the back and looked her over. "You're too thin, I don't know what he thinks I am going to be able to do with you. Come in here."

She walked Maka into a back room, the dancers were getting themselves ready, older women were rude to the younger girls, a couple of them cutting lines of cocaine, and a young girl called out "Mother." The woman looked at Maka, "Wait here, don't move."

Maka watched her walk over to the young girl and began observing as much as she could around the room. Looking for the girls, she noticed there were some private stalls around the corner, a hanging rack with outfits for the dancers, some with sequins, and some that looked like just strings hanging on a hanger. She needed to find where the newer girls would be. She didn't think they would be just walking around in the backroom freely with the other girls. The new girls tended to be a flight risk and the 'Daddy' would not take a chance on losing a profit that way. She was hoping Alan was having better luck.

***

The large man that once stood in the hallway near Alan was now banging on the door of the room Alan was next to. He heard him say "You have three minutes man."

Alan knew he would be banging on his door next. He had to think fast and made a quick decision. Not sure if it was the right one, he decided to show the young girl a picture of Aiyana.

"Have you seen this girl?"

She looked at the picture. "Maybe. Why? Are you a cop?"

"No. No. Where have you seen her?

"What's it worth to you?"

Suddenly the quiet, scared girl that she appeared to be when Alan first came in was more confident than she had let on. Alan pulled a fifty-dollar bill out of his pocket. She snatched it immediately, and sat back on the cot, hiding the money in her thong.

"Don't tell Daddy you gave that to me."

"Don't tell him I asked you about this girl."

She nodded. "I saw her, in one of the rooms down the hall. They were going to take her to Mother before you came."

"Who's Mother?"

"She takes care of us, kind of. She spends more time with the dancers though."

A loud bang on the door. "Two minutes man."

"Do you want to be here?"

"Of course not, trying to save money to square up."

The door flung open; the tour guide stood there waiting for Alan. "Let's go, times up."

Alan followed the tour guide and said, "I would like to go back to the club for a drink."

"Sure, Señor."

***

Maka found herself in a daunting position and was trying to quickly figure it out. There were several girls in the room changing and getting ready to go out to dance. Still no sign of Aiyana.

Mother walked over to her, "You're not the right fit for my customers. Leave."

Maka was surprised and relieved at the same time.

"But Señora, I need the money."

"Not my problem. You tell T to take you someplace else."

Maka tried to walk around a bit more, looking for the girls.

Mother yelled to her, "Hey! Get out!"

Maka began to walk back through observing all she could. She couldn't help but wonder where the girls could be. She was hoping Alan was OK and having better luck. She lingered as long as she could in the back of the house trying to blend in to get closer. She noticed another hallway, no one was around or paying much attention to her. She decided to try exploring where it led.

***

In the club, Alan leaned against the end of the bar, he had paid for his fifteen minutes and his tour guide was already bringing in another sex tourist. The bartender leaned over to Alan, "You can't stand there unless you're drinking. What'll it be?"

Alan looked around, "Top shelf tequila," he felt at this point he could use another drink. Watching the bartender pour his drink a familiar face caught his eye. The bartender slid his drink to him, "Eighteen dollars." Alan, distracted from trying to put a name to a face, reached into his wallet, and gave the bartender a twenty. Sipping on his tequila he watched the tall Native American man walk towards the stage, smoking a skinny cigar, he looked him over, seeing his boots. As he sipped on his drink it hit him; it was Chief Hurd!

Thinking to himself, *What the hell is he doing here?* he watched as Hurd sat down with three other men, mostly talking, not watching the dancers.

Alan started talking to himself, *Why would he be here? And where is Maka?*

Hurd was sitting with three men, one also seemed very familiar to Alan. He watched from the shadows of the bar, hoping they wouldn't see him. Keeping an eye out for Maka, he tried his phone again. This time he had two bars show up, he tried to text her, typing "Where are you? I haven't found her. At the bar. Hurd is here." He hit send. He decided to try and walk past the table to hear what they were talking about. He slammed his drink to muster up the courage to try and get closer without being seen. Since Hurd had his back to him, he thought it might be easier. He made his way through the cluster of men waving their dollar bills at the dancers and was able to sit in a spot adjacent to their table. The club was so loud he could hardly hear what the men were talking about, he picked up a word here and there. He thought he heard him say something about all going to Tenancingo, more money, turn over to pollero. One of the men raised his voice and they began to argue. Alan felt he better go back into the shadows and not risk the Chief seeing him. He got up quickly and stood back at the end of the bar.

After what seemed like hours, but was only minutes that went by, the Chief looked frustrated and stood up. The other men stood up as well, they pointed to the hidden door Alan had come through and started walking that way. Alan didn't know what to do, he didn't want to be seen and still hadn't heard from Maka. He inched his way deeper into the corner of the bar where it was the darkest. He watched the three men walk to the door. Still trying to place the one, he thought who it might be, he decided to google it. It was a rapper from LA whose career was taking off.

What the hell is going on? Alan thought to himself, never having been exposed to this before, he heard stories but never experienced the severity of it.

***

Maka was walking the hallway not knowing in what direction she was going anymore. It was dark as she started to pass some of the booths. She could hear the activities going on inside them. She tried to investigate them as she passed, hoping to see Aiyana, but only saw men with their pants around their ankles and emotionless girls enslaved to things they weren't even mature enough to know about. A man came from around the corner followed by a young Caucasian girl. He stopped Maka, "Saw you in the back, did Mother send you down here?"

"Yes, she told me to get out of there and pointed this way." Maka looked at the young girl, who appeared to have been crying, and wouldn't make eye contact with her. She kept her head down.

"Go to the Clock Watcher, he will show you where to go. I will be back in a bit."

Maka kept walking, passing booth after booth, she lost count of how many she passed. Once the man was out of sight, she tried her cell phone and saw she had no service.

She could hear some men talking ahead, so she stayed back, they were coming her way. She saw an empty booth with a curtain and slipped inside.

As the men came closer, she could see their shoes under the curtain as they passed. A pair of cowboy boots appeared, and she thought, *I know those boots.* She tried to peek through the curtain but could only see the back of their heads. Taking advantage of this time to slip out, she continued.

***

Alan was still hiding at the bar; he could feel sweat beading on his upper lip. All he could do is think how much he wanted out of this place. The lights flickered in the bar and the stage changed colors. They seemed to be bringing out new girls and the ones that were on stage went in the back. Some new waitresses started working the room as well, only wearing a g-string. Alan kept a lookout for Maka. Trying not to panic and feeling abandoned by her, he didn't know if he should go look for her, go back to the car or stay where he was. He was just a writer; he wasn't trained for this kind of work or situation. He started to rethink volunteering to help her, but it was a little late to leave now.

Bouncers rushed past the bar toward the stage, several men had jumped on the stage and were trying to dance with the girls. The room exploded into chaos, fights were breaking out, tables were overturned, and men punching each other in the face. A few girls ran to the back room, while the girls off to the side continued to dance as if nothing was happening. With all the commotion Alan saw an opportunity to slip through the hidden door with hopes to find Maka. He couldn't just stand there any longer doing nothing. He saw some men walk through the door, he followed close behind.

***

Walking along the wall of the hallway, Maka found herself coming up on some light ahead that illuminated the room she was about to enter. There was a very large man standing by a door, she assumed this must be the 'Clock Watcher' they mentioned. Several men were standing around, some with a glass of bourbon, others holding beer bottles, the place was herb friendly, she could smell the overwhelming odor of marijuana.

A door flew open, and a man came out yelling with his hands covering his genitals appearing to be crying a little bit and angry at the same time "Stupid bitch bit me! Someone call an ambulance!" He was very dramatic.

"I think she could have rabies or whatever it is they have!"

One of the men turned and caught a glimpse of Maka, she quickly slipped into the room the man just stormed out of. A young girl appeared to be cowering in the corner. Maka closed the door behind her, she kept an eye on the door and an eye on the girl.

"Who the fuck are you!" the girl growled.

"What happened? Why is the man freaking out?"

"I bit him, have a problem with that?"

She looked up at Maka, her face bruised, blood dripping from her nose, a small cut over her lip.

"Are you OK?" Maka slowly approached her to get a better look. The girl's long black hair covered her face.

"I'm fine." She tried to speak but began to vomit. The door flew open, it was the Clock Watcher. He started to walk towards the young girl. When she finished vomiting, she pushed her hair back, and that was when Maka saw Aiyana.

The Clock Watcher was pissed off, "Get the fuck up!"

Maka stepped in between, "I got this, taking her to Mother."

"Mother sent you?"

"Yeah, and you know how pissed she gets if you keep her waiting. Do you want to deal with her?"

He looked angry and ready to explode, the veins were popping out of his neck, and his eyes looked buggy. "Clean her up! She's got a date."

"Ok. I will take her to Mother." She stood, helping Aiyana up.

The Clock Watcher stood blocking the door.

Maka stopped and looked him in the eyes.

"Can you move?"

He moved slightly to the side. The girls walked out, Aiyana was unstable and Maka had to help her walk down the hallway.

"Where are you taking me, bitch?"

"Stop talking and keep walking."

"Not until you tell me where the fuck you are taking me you stupid bitch."

"Aiyana, shut up and keep walking."

She stopped for a brief second and looked Maka in the eyes.

"How do you know my name?"

She whispered, "If you want to get out of here keep walking," she nodded and kept pace with Maka.

***

Alan couldn't believe it. He had ended up back where he had started. He was standing in the middle of the room listening to the man whine about being bitten. The man went on and on about how a feral native girl was wild and how he tried to tame her. Alan's patience had been wearing thin and he wasn't sure how much more he could listen to or watch this.

The man went on and on "You should have seen how this wild Indian struggled. I was getting my money's worth with her until the bitch bit me."

One of the other men spoke up, "Where is she? I'd like to see if I can tame the wild cat."

A man appeared out of nowhere, Alan hadn't seen him before. He went on to say, "Gentlemen, if you would be so kind to follow us to the next room for drinks on the house, while we help Mr. Smith with his injury." The men seemed to calm down when they heard "free drinks." "Two men can help escort Mr. Smith for medical help."

Alan could hear the Clock Watcher and this new man speaking. "Where did that little bitch go?"

"She went off with the new girl."

"What new girl?"

"I don't know, one of T's girls. She took her to Mother."

"I'll deal with T later. Get that room cleaned up *now*."

Sarcastically he replied, "Si, *señor.*"

Alan wondered if the new girl could be Maka. He decided to go in the direction they mentioned she went. He walked cautiously down the hallway hoping to run into her. He heard someone coming out of the shadows, a large man bumped into him.

"Sorry, man."

Alan looked, it was the rapper and luckily, he was alone.

"Yeah," is all Alan could think to say as they passed. Then Alan spoke up, "This is the way back to the club, right?"

"Straight ahead, man."

***

Maka was in a difficult position, her mind was racing. She had to come up with a plan quickly to get all of them out safely. She knew she would only have one shot to get Aiyana out. How would she find Alan and where is Dakota? They were getting closer to the door of the dressing room. Maka didn't know any other way out.

"We need to get my bag."

"Leave it."

"No, I need it. You have to get my bag."

"Where is it?"

"Back room."

"Where Mother is?"

"Yes."

"No. No way. We need to get out of here."

"That's the only way out unless you want to go through the club."

"The only way is through the back room. Great."

Maka started walking. "OK. Follow my lead. Don't say anything."

Aiyana was getting weaker; whatever kind of drugs they had given her were starting to kick in.

"Aiyana, where is Dakota?"

She was foggy, Maka's voice sounded so far away like they were in a tunnel.

Maka stopped walking and looked her in the eye, "Aiyana are you OK? Can you hear me?"

She nodded her head. "Where is your friend? Where is Dakota? Talk to me."

Aiyana tried to speak "I don't…know…I think she is dead." She began to cry.

Maka gave her a little shake, trying to snap her out of it. "We will find her. First, let's get you out of here, do you know a better way?"

She pointed to the left of them, Maka had not come from that way, she hesitated. "Are you sure?"

Aiyana was weak, Maka knew she needed to get her to the car.

They walked toward the exit she pointed out and could hear the chaos in the club. They found themselves at the end of the hallway but couldn't find the door, it all blended as one. She struggled to try to find a way out when suddenly the door flew open, almost knocking them to the ground. She got them into the back room, the girls were running out the back door. Aiyana found her bag as Maka was trying to hurry her. She saw chaos breaking out all over the place, thankfully no sign of the mother. People were scattering everywhere; they took the opportunity to make their way to the street. The *policia* arrived, trying to break up the fights. Maka was able to tuck into the stampede of people making their way out of the club.

***

Unknowingly, Alan was not far behind them when two men who worked there came rushing up behind, opening the curtains on the booths. They appeared to be looking for someone, pulling back the curtains, infuriating the men inside.

"What the fuck, man. Close it!"

Alan couldn't wait to get out of there, he looked franticly for Maka but there was no sign of her, the crowd was forcing him outside. The streets seemed even more chaotic than inside the club.

The *policia* was everywhere, breaking up fights, and herding people to different areas. He pushed through the wall of people heading in the direction of their car.

Caught up in the rush, he didn't realize he walked past Chief Hurd who was standing off to the side with one of the men he was with earlier. As Alan walked past him, Hurd stopped talking and recognized him, he tried to follow, but a crowd of people cut him off, causing him to lose sight of Alan.

***

Maka made it to the car and was helping Aiyana into the backseat, she was beginning to lose muscle control and become foggy from the drugs.

Alan stopped to check if he had cell service, noticing he did, he tried to call Maka.

Hurd now had Alan in his view again, he continued to follow him.

Maka was on the phone with the forensic agent. "I need you to email me the paperwork now, we can't wait and set up the safe house, she will need a doctor. Call the Chief CBP and let him know we are coming. I'll call you back."

She saw Alan was calling and answered, "Where are you? Are you OK?" he could hear the stress in her voice.

"I'm trying to find the car. Where are you? Are you OK? I didn't find Aiyana."

"I found her. I just put her in the car. Describe where you are, and I will try to guide you in."

"I think I got turned around."

"That's OK. Just tell me what you see. I'll stand next to the car."

"I'm next to a sign that says La Zone Norte on the corner, club Revolution."

"You're close, just keep going, and you will see the car."

***

So many people, a sea of many cultures of all ages filled the streets, Alan kept looking for Maka. Moments later he saw Hurd standing across the street to his right staring at him. He looked to his left and saw the car. He didn't know what to do. Alan saw him looking toward the direction of the car. Hurd was alone now, not knowing what to do, Alan texted Maka trying to alert her.

The crowd seemed to be in their favor once again as he blended in, disappearing from Hurd's view. Alan walked against the stampede of people toward the car. People were shoving each other and blocking the streets and sidewalks. Cars were at a standstill, honking and trying to crawl through the street.

Alan got close enough to Maka and spoke out to her, "Hurd is here."

"I know, we need to get in the car!" Maka yelled at Alan, he raced to the passenger front door, looked into the backseat, and saw Aiyana unconscious. Maka had the car started and in drive before he could close the door.

Hurd reunited with one of the other men, they were pushing their way through the crowd.

"They have the girl! Don't let them cross the border."

Looking in the backseat, Alan was concerned.

"Is she alright?"

The wheels screeched as Maka accelerated, looking in the rear-view mirror she could see the Chief flailing his arms and hitting the man.

Akéšakpe

16

Stuck in traffic, Maka took a moment to assess the situation, handing her phone to Alan.

"Check to see if there is anything from Barton."

"Yes, there is a message from her. It says you are set at the border."

In the backseat Aiyana is starting to regain a little bit of consciousness, still coming in and out. Alan looks back to check on her.

"How is she doing?"

"She's out again."

"Director made the call himself."

"Thank god!" Alan replied to her, both observed their surroundings and watched to see if they were being followed.

"I have a feeling they aren't going to make it easy for us to get to the CBX."

Maka tried to reach for her bag behind the seat, it was just out of her reach. Alan reached over and picks it up, passing it to her.

"Thanks. Can you grab my shoes? I need to get out of these heels."

He hands her a pair of black tennis shoes; she slips off the heels and carefully puts on the shoes while she drives.

"Can you hand me that jacket?"

Alan handed her a red sweatshirt jacket, she put it on trying to cover the dress she was wearing.

Reaching into the glove box, she pulled out her credentials and gun.

"Put this in my bag," she handed the gun to Alan.

Turning onto the SR 905, the traffic was bumper to bumper.

"We are almost there, grab that bottle of water and see if you can get her to wake up. She's still lethargic; you may need to shake her out of it a bit."

Alan reached over and gently tried to wake her. He wasn't getting much of a response; he tried pouring water in his hand and lightly splashed it on her face. That seemed to help, she started to come to.

"Can you sit up? Drink some of this," he handed her the bottle of water.

She slowly slid up the backseat, could barely hold the bottle of water, attempted to take a sip and spilled it down her front.

"Keep drinking," Alan sat back in his seat.

"Aiyana we are almost to the border; I need you to be able to walk with us. Can you understand me?"

Maka looked over her shoulder; Aiyana nodded, sipping on the water.

"Are we going home?"

"Yes." Maka parked the car.

"We made it!" Alan had a sigh of relief.

"Not yet."

There was a look of concern and disappointment on his face.

"We need to get to the US Customs office. They will take us to the safe house in San Diego first."

Alan gathered the bags.

"Aiyana, I will come around and help you out. We will need to move fast."

Aiyana dropped the water bottle to the floor and re-positioned herself. Maka looked at Alan.

"Ready?"

They jumped out of the car, and opening the back door, Maka scanned the area. As Aiyana was coming out of the car, a black SUV with blacked-out windows was speeding toward them. Maka knew it had to be the Chief or the cartel.

"We have to go! They're coming."

In a state of panic, they started to run to the entrance of the CBX.

Aiyana stumbled, Alan tried to help her and carry the bags. The SUV came to a screeching stop, two men jumped out of the back and were running toward them. Maka ran with Aiyana, pushing her to go faster, reaching the door she opened it, getting them inside. She wasn't sure which way to go.

"Keep going!"

"Which way?" Alan frantically yelled to her.

"Straight over there, Customs."

They were approaching the counter when Maka heard her name.

"Maka, this way!"

She turned and saw several U.S. agents just as the men from the SUV were getting closer.

The agents directed them to a private office. The men stopped in their tracks, immediately turned, and went back.

The office was cold, the agents were circling everywhere, they had Alan and Aiyana sit in a conference room area. Aiyana clutched her bag, shivering. Someone came in with a blanket for her.

"We had someone run over to the gift shop to get you something warm to wear."

Aiyana covered herself with the blanket. Maka was most concerned to get them to the safe house and as far from the border as she could. Alan watched as she seemed to be fighting with one of the agents. He wasn't sure what to say to Aiyana, he had many questions running through his head.

"Do you need anything?"

"No. I just want to go home."

"I understand. Maka is very resourceful, she will make sure you are safe and taken care of."

An agent came in with coffee, sandwiches, and snacks. He put them down on the table in front of them.

"It will be just a few more minutes. Have something to eat."

Alan watched Maka pacing and yelling at whoever that agent was she was talking to. She looked upset and came storming into the conference room.

"Are you OK?" Alan asked.

"No. We need to get out of here and they are insisting on detaining us before taking us to the safe house. I have a call into the Director.

"Why couldn't we just all leave and walk through the bridge back to San Diego?" Alan asked.

"It doesn't work that way. Please eat something, both of you." She walked back out of the room and closed the door behind her.

"Would you prefer turkey or ham?"

"I'm not hungry."

"Neither am I, but you need to eat. It will help you feel better."

Aiyana looked at the sandwiches and slid the turkey in front of her. Alan opened a bag of chips and placed it in front of her. He struggled with wanting to eat, stressed, he sipped on the coffee.

"How are you feeling?"

"Like I was run over a hundred times or more." She picked at her sandwich, taking tiny bites.

"Eating will help you feel better, whatever drugs they were giving you, some food in your stomach will help."

She nodded in agreement; her throat held a huge lump in it as she fought back tears. She was scared and traumatized, a little in shock.

"What's going to happen to me now?"

"Maka is working everything out, you're safe now."

Aiyana began to cry; Alan wasn't sure what to do. He saw a box of Kleenex across the room and went and brought the box to her.

Maka was trying to make arrangements to get them back to San Diego, but the Policia Federal officers were blocking her from connecting with the Director. She had to meet their demands and pay them five thousand dollars to be able to cross through the CBX to San Diego. The only person she felt she could trust was the Director. She stepped aside to take a call to debrief him quickly on their efforts to get help.

The Director assured Maka they would have everything set for them to arrive safely back in the U.S.

Akéšakowiŋ

17

Darkness fell over the small, isolated one-story cedar home, the sound of the ocean waves was breaking on the nearby beach. A black van with no rear windows drove up to the cottage, tucked away hidden behind trees.

The van circled around to the back of the home and pulled into the three-car attached garage, closing its door behind them. An armed man jumped out of the front driver's side of the van, dressed in a black t-shirt, bullet-resistant vest, black cargo pants and military-style boots. Walking to the rear of the van, he opened the doors. Maka, Alan, and Aiyana had fallen asleep; they were sitting comfortably in the back.

"Home sweet home." The man held the door open while they all climbed out.

"Not necessary, Reed." Maka gave him a look.

Maka felt a combined sense of relief and elation creep over her, they were safer here.

They walked through the house, exhausted, looking for someplace to rest. Alan helped carry the bags, dropping them at the end of the hallway.

"Now what?" he said looking intently at Maka.

"Aiyana, let me show you to your room and get you settled. Alan, help yourself to something in the kitchen. I will be right back."

They walked down the hallway to one of the four bedrooms. It was a simple house, each bedroom had a bathroom, bed, and dresser. The floors throughout the home were mostly hardwood, it was lightly decorated, didn't have a lot of furniture but enough that they could be comfortable. For Aiyana, compared to all she had been through, this was five-star quality.

"This will be your room. We will get you some clothes tomorrow and you will see the doctor."

"You never told me how you knew my name."

"We can talk about it in the morning. You need to rest."

"I need to know."

"If I tell you, do you promise to go to bed, and we can talk more in the morning?"

"OK."

Maka started to walk out of the bedroom and then stopped.

"Your brother Paythan helped lead us to you. He is quite the young man."

"You know Paythan? Where is he? Can I see him?"

"You promised. We can talk more in the morning. Good night."

"But wait."

Maka closed the bedroom door. She could hear a faint "Night."

Alan was going through the kitchen cupboards and looking through the refrigerator.

"Find anything?"

He jumped, slamming the door. Maka startled him, he turned quickly.

"Guess I'm still a little on edge. Long day."

She walked closer to him.

"Are you OK? This is the first time we have been able to talk since we have been back."

"I know. I'm OK. It all seems so surreal. I'm a writer and not in a million years would I have ever been able to imagine, let alone find words and write to describe what I just witnessed, and how it felt."

"The world isn't always what you think it is. There's a secret world out there."

Alan stepped closer to Maka and hugged her tight. He wasn't sure if he wanted to cry or hold onto her and never let her go.

"Aiyana asked how I knew her. I had to tell her Paythan, but I couldn't tell her anything tonight. She's been through enough; I didn't want to tell her."

"Probably better you didn't. I can be there when you do."

Maka broke the hug and started to walk away a bit.

"I need to shower and look over some paperwork. Let me show you to your room."

Alan felt a little puzzled that she had said,"Your room." He had been looking forward to being with her, just holding her after all they had been through.

"Well wait, what's next? How do I get home?"

"You can't go home yet, Alan. They are looking for all of us. We need to stay here until I get further notice. It is too dangerous for you to go home now."

"I need to call my agent."

"You can't, no one can know where you are. No internet, no phones for you."

"Maka, when you asked me to come, and I agreed, this was not in the plan."

"I know Alan, I truly am sorry."

"I am too, I can't stay here, my career is on the line."

Maka took Alan by the hand and led him down the hallway to the furthest room from Aiyana's. The master bedroom had a king-size bed and 55-inch television.

"Can we please talk about it in the morning? We will be able to work it out, I promise. You won't jeopardize your career or your work." She kissed him on the cheek. "I need to shower. You can use this bathroom; I will go to the other."

She left the room. Alan walked into the bathroom, removing his clothes, just dropping them on the floor, and he stepped into the shower. Leaning up against the wall, hot water bouncing off of him, he submerged his head under the water and began to cry. It started as just tears that lead to sobbing, he thought to himself he couldn't recall a time he ever cried like that, the steam filled the shower and spilled out into the room.

Maka brought her bag into the bathroom, she turned on the shower to let it run. She started to undress and saw her reflection in the mirror, she stopped for a moment looking deeply into her eyes, searching her soul. She had a look of disappointment in herself, stepped into the shower and instantly began to cry. She sobbed so hard she had to sit on the shower floor. She was overwhelmed with emotions. So many things rushed through her mind, rehashing what she could have done better and what she did that was wrong. The overwhelming guilt and memories of her childhood, and her sister's tragic death, were all triggered.

By the time she got out of the shower and made it back to the master bedroom, Alan was lying asleep in bed with his laptop open to his screenplay. She slowly closed his door and went to the adjacent room, crawled into bed, turned on the light on the nightstand, pulled out her computer, and began trying to write her report. She finally succumbed to the tiredness in her limbs, set her computer aside, her eyes slowly closed, and she too drifted into a peaceful sleep. There was much work to do; it would take time, but that could wait until tomorrow.

Morning came quickly, the sun streamed golden through the cracks of the blinds. Maka was sitting at the counter in the kitchen working on her laptop. Aiyana came in still wearing the sweatshirt and sweatpants they gave her at the CBX.

"Good morning. Coffee?" Maka stood and walked towards the coffee pot.

"Sure."

"Sleep OK?"

"Better than I have in weeks."

Maka placed the coffee cup and creamer on the island between them. Aiyana sat on one of the stools.

"Hungry?"

"No, where's Paythan? Is he coming?"

Maka walked back to the coffee pot to fill her cup, she felt a pit in her stomach and a lump grew in her throat. She had a flashback memory of when she was told her sister was killed. She didn't know how to tell Aiyana.

"No, He's not. He was very worried about you."

Maka stood at the island.

"He knows you found me, right?"

"Paythan came to look for you on his own. Because of the clues he left we were able to find you. There is no easy way to tell you, sweetie, Paythan is dead."

Aiyana stood up immediately.

"You're lying. No, he's not! We were going to move in together. We had plans." She started to cry. "I don't believe you; I want to go see him. Now!"

She raced to the front door.

"Aiyana, stop."

She tried to open it, but it was locked from the inside.

"*Open the door!*" she yelled.

Alan heard the crying and was standing in the hallway; he didn't know what to do. Maka motioned him to stay there, she walked over to try and hug Aiyana.

Aiyana pushed her away and slid down the door onto the floor, crying. Maka knew there were no words that were going to help her right now, she sat down next to her hoping to bring some comfort. She placed her arm around her, and Aiyana buried her face into Maka's shoulder. She began to sob. Maka held her, she could feel the tears touch her skin through her shirt. They sat in silence for what felt like hours, Alan went back to his room.

Maka helped Aiyana back up and walked her to her room.

"Rest for a bit, you have been through so much. I will make you something to eat."

Aiyana lay in bed crying, As Maka closed the door she could hear her sobbing so hard she could hardly catch her breath. Maka stood at the door for a moment, wondering if she should go back in or give her some space.

Alan approached her in the hallway, embracing her in a comforting hug.

He whispered, "Is she OK?"

"She will be."

"Are you OK?"

"I'm fine."

"She should rest a bit. Let me make you something to eat."

Alan kept his arm around Maka as they walked to the kitchen. He pulled a chair out for her.

"Sit, I will get you a fresh cup of coffee. You need to eat something."

Alan placed a cup of coffee and orange juice in front of Maka.

"Thank you. You don't have to do this."

Alan smiled and started going through the refrigerator.

"Did I do the right thing, Alan?" Maka put her face in her hands. "Should I have waited to tell her about Paythan?"

He closed the refrigerator door, not satisfied with the choices.

"I don't think you had any other choice. There is never a good time to tell someone they lost a loved one."

There were moments of silence. Maka played with her cup for a bit. There was a knock at the door, startling Alan.

"Who knows we are here?" he asked.

"There are only three other agents beside me who know where we are. The doctor is supposed to come. I'm sure it's one of them."

Maka checked the security camera, there were two women, one wearing sunglasses, a white shirt, and dark pants, the other wearing a golf shirt, holding a black bag. Alan, thinking to himself, *God, I'm living one of my movies.*

"It's McKenzie and the doctor."

Maka brought her and the doctor into the kitchen to meet Alan. She was an attractive, stylish woman of substance with long sandy blond hair pulled back and a white shirt, a penchant for dark, custom-tailored pants, and her government-issued Glock on her side.

"Alan this is Agent McKenzie."

"Nice to meet you, Alan."

"Pleasure to meet you."

The other woman stepped around the back of McKenzie.

"This is Doctor Williams. She is part of a special team for victims," McKenzie introduced her.

"Hi. So, where is she?" Williams asked.

"Follow me, she is in her room." Maka led the doctor to Aiyana's room, "Let me tell her you are here; she was still coming out of the drugs last night."

Williams stepped aside to give her some space. Maka tapped on the door, "Aiyana are you awake?" She didn't hear anything, they tried to knock again, and still no response. Maka slowly opened the door and saw Aiyana fast asleep.

"Should we wake her?"

"Yes, they only gave me a certain time to be here." Maka and the doctor walked into the room and gently woke her.

"Aiyana, how are you feeling?"

She was slowly coming to, rubbing her eyes. "I forgot where I was."

"That's good you were sleeping so well."

Aiyana saw Williams in the doorway holding a black bag. She sat up quickly.

"This is Dr. Williams. Remember last night I mentioned you would be seeing a doctor? I am going to leave the two of you alone. If you need me,

I'll be in the kitchen." Aiyana was scared and Maka could see the look on her face. "You are in good hands." She pulled the covers up over her, almost to her neck.

"Hi Aiyana, is it OK if I just take some of your vitals? I'm concerned about what kind of drugs they may have given you." Williams looked at Maka who slowly was leaving the room, closing the door behind her.

Maka found McKenzie and asked her to step into her bedroom briefly.

"Did the Director read my report from last night?"

"Yes, that's why he sent me. This is big Maka. You are accusing the Chief of Police of one of the largest reservations."

"Not accusing, he was there. The evidence is there."

"Your biggest witnesses are a seventeen-year-old girl and a college professor. You know we will need more."

"I have more." Maka paced the room. "We need to keep her under our protection until we bring him in."

"Where is he?"

"As of yesterday, Tijuana. I debriefed the agents at the border, and Carrol and Bynes took the information. They were supposed to be checking the airlines, and private airports and have border patrol on the lookout."

She walked over to her bag and pulled out a folder. "Here, take this and give it to the Director. I have copies, it's more evidence to expedite if they have him contained in Mexico."

McKenzie flipped through the folder. "No one passed along any information from yesterday. That's partly why they sent me today."

"I had to pay off the Mexicans, five grand of my own money so they would let us take Aiyana with us."

"First I'm hearing about that too."

"I can't believe this!" Maka started to pace, getting angry.

"I think Hurd would go back to the Reservation; he will feel safer there."

"That would be ludicrous."

"Think about it Maka, if he pissed off whoever he is working with in Tijuana, they won't stand for that, no loose ends."

"Right."

"We don't know how respected he is with them. And knowing Hurd, my guess is not very."

"Who can we trust to send to the Res?"

"No one, you and I."

"What about Autumn? She did come and warn me."

McKenzie tossed the folder back on Maka's bed.

"Your call. She could tip him off."

"Or she could help us." Maka picked up her cell phone.

The doctor approached Alan in the kitchen, "Excuse me do you have any orange juice or bottled water?"

"Oh, yes. Let me get it, how is she?" Alan asked as he poured the juice.

"Weak, dehydrated, having a few withdrawals. She will need to drink something this morning, to keep her hydrated."

"Thank you."

"Let me know if there is anything I can do to help. Should I fix her something to eat now?

"I would wait until she comes out."

Williams returned to Aiyana's room. Alan sat at the table on his laptop as he waited for Maka.

Moments later Maka, McKenzie, and Dr. Williams walked into the kitchen.

"She has been through some of the worst trauma I have seen in a while. She will need counseling as soon as possible and a lot of liquids. She is extremely dehydrated and malnourished. As you know, they practically starve these kids. She will be detoxing for days; I will get in touch with the blood results tomorrow. This is for nausea, and these are for the STI. Please make sure she takes these as prescribed on the bottle. She has a strong spirit; she will be OK."

"Thank you, doctor." Maka reached for a bottle of medication from the doctor.

"We should go." McKenzie led Williams to the door.

Maka locked the door behind them and let out a big sigh. Alan was speechless, he had never experienced anything like this and wasn't sure what to say or do. He wanted to save them both but didn't know how.

"How about I make us all some breakfast now?'

Maka nodded and poured another cup of coffee.

"I should check on Aiyana." As she said that, Aiyana walked into the kitchen.

"How are you feeling?"

"Like I could sleep for a year."

Alan set a cup of orange juice in front of her.

"Any coffee?"

He turned and poured her a cup.

"Juice and water would be better," he said, setting down the coffee.

Aiyana sipped the coffee; she could hardly hold up her head.

"Are you an agent, too?"

Alan was multi-tasking, scrambling eggs, "No. I was Paythan's teacher at USC. I'm so sorry for your loss."

He poured her another glass of orange juice and brought it to her.

"Do you know what happened?" she played with her glass. "Wait, are you the writing teacher?"

"Yes."

"He mentioned you. He said you were nice to him."

She pushed the glass away from her. Alan walked over and slid it gently back in front of her.

"You need to eat a little something. It will help."

Aiyana looked frustrated at Alan. "Why are you here?"

Alan placed the bread in the toaster and continued cooking. Maka spoke for him.

"I asked him to help me."

Alan slid the breakfast he made for Aiyana across the counter, fluffy scrambled eggs, a couple of pieces of bacon, and toast.

"Please eat something, you will feel better with some protein."

She played with the eggs with her fork, picking at them, trying to take a small bite.

"What did Paythan tell you about me?" Alan picked up his cup of coffee and leaned against the counter to talk with her.

"He liked you a lot. He said you were one of the only teachers that understood him and helped him." She started to eat slowly. "He looked up to you."

"I had no idea."

"Ya know, he was coming to the Res to get me. I was going to come back to California to live with him."

"I didn't know that." Alan refilled her coffee cup and his.

"Yeah, he was going to help me get into USC."

"You want to go to college there? What do you want to major in?"

"Teaching, so I can be a teacher on the Res. Teachers quit and we don't have very many, so kids don't go to school. I want to teach our traditions and about the world."

"That sounds incredible, Aiyana."

"Please tell me what happened to my brother." She looked Maka dismally in the eyes.

Maka poured herself a fresh cup of coffee and walked closer to Aiyana. Maka's mind raced with thoughts as she hesitated in telling her what happened. She didn't feel she was emotionally stable after all she went through and yet she knew when it was her sister, she needed answers. She took a deep breath.

"We don't know for sure exactly what happened. What I do know is he was found in Tijuana, not far from the red district, beaten. The Mexican authorities tried to say it was motorcycle related. But it was clear in the autopsy, he was beaten. I believe he came looking for you and possibly found you. But…"

Aiyana tried to hold back the tears and all the emotions welling up inside her. She was becoming nauseous and shoved her plate as far away as she could.

"I don't understand."

Maka sat next to her, Alan fixed Maka's plate and placed it down. He felt the best way for him to show up was to stay silent and supportive.

Maka put her hand on Aiyana's shoulder. "Do you feel up to telling me how you ended up in Tijuana?"

Aiyana sat in silence for a moment. She was trying to find the strength to tell them what happened.

"Was it the night of the protest?" Maka asked.

"Yes, Chayton left Dakota and me at the gas station right on the edge of the Res. He said he would be back. We waited for over an hour and he never came. Those skinheads were making us nervous; Dakota was freaked out by them. We stayed inside waiting and Chief Hurd came in and asked us what we were doing. Dakota told him and he offered us a ride home. He said he needed to make a stop; it was an old hotel. He asked us to come inside with him, so we did. It didn't feel right, the whole time I felt sick to my stomach, and I told Dakota we should have waited for Chayton or Paythan."

Alan pulled up a high-top stool and sat with them around the island.

"What happened when you went inside?"

Aiyana started to get uncomfortable and fidget. Maka watched as she played with her fingers behind her back.

"There was an older guy, an Indian, and two younger black men. They all knew each other, they were drinking. Chief Hurd helped himself to a drink and offered us one. Dakota took one, I told him no. I don't drink. They started to play music, one of the guys was a musician or rapper, I think. I asked when we were going to leave, but they wouldn't tell me. I tried to call Paythan, but my cell phone didn't work there. The Chief just kept saying soon, then a couple of other girls came out from one of the rooms and started drinking and partying with the men. One of the girls tried to get me to drink with them. She was nice at first but when I wouldn't dance with them, she got mad at me, started saying mean things to me. Dakota danced with them and drank with them.

One of the girls tried to be nice to me and brought me water. I kept asking if we could go, and they repeated themselves saying soon and that I needed to relax. One of the men took the mean girl into a room, I never saw them again."

"When did you leave for Tijuana?"

"I don't know for sure, the last thing I remember was Dakota was acting strange she looked like she passed out, then the next thing I remember was waking up on a dirty mat in a dark room, it had a dirt floor. I don't know how long we were in there. I think they drugged us."

"Was Dakota in the room with you?"

"Yes, but I couldn't wake her up." Aiyana started to get uncomfortable.

"Was she breathing?"

"Yes."

Maka turned to her, "I know this is hard sweetie. Do you want to take a break?"

"No. I don't know how we got to Tijuana. Someone came into that room, and I tried to fight, I screamed, kicked, and tried to get out of there.

He was strong, he gave me a shot and that's when I woke in Mexico."

"Did you ever see Chief Hurd again after that night?"

Aiyana looked over at Alan, he sat in silence with the most empathetic look in his eyes. It was comforting to Aiyana.

"Once. He came into the room and looked at me like he owned me. Told me to be a good girl and do what I was told."

Aiyana began to feel sick.

"I don't feel well." She jumped and ran to the bathroom.

Alan instinctively followed behind to make sure she was OK. Maka followed him.

"Do you think it was too much?" he asked.

"Maybe, I needed the information. There is no easy way around it."

They stood outside the bathroom door. Alan tapped lightly on the door. "Aiyana, are you OK?"

She didn't answer, they could hear her crying. Alan knocked again. Still no answer.

Maka reflected again on how she felt with her sister, she gently took Alan by the arm. "Let's give her some time alone."

Maka excused herself for a moment, "I need to call the office, I will meet you in the kitchen in a bit."

Maka went to her bedroom and called McKenzie. "Hey, we got it. Aiyana identified Hurd. Did you get the CCTV recordings from the gas station?"

"Yes"

"Well, what did you see?"

"I emailed you the link, look for yourself. Tell me what you see."

Maka pulled out her laptop, logged in, and found the link. "Standby."

She finally began to watch the video, it revealed the skinheads causing issues in the parking lot, she scrubbed through to the SUV that Aiyana and Dakota got into. Sure, enough it shows Chief Hurd driving it, he got out and came back with the girls.

"We got 'em!" Maka blurted out in excitement.

"Well possibly, we still have some red tape to get through."

"No way, this is a slam dunk. It's even better evidence than "Operation New Beginning.""

"Maka, we will need the Missing Child Unit, Fugitive Task Force and work with local authorities."

"Set it up! We uncovered allegations of sex trafficking, we have evidence. Call and set up the task force and let's go get the son of a bitch. I will submit the paperwork while you make the calls."

Later that evening Alan and Maka sat at the kitchen table, sipping on tea. Aiyana came into the room slowly, her hair unbrushed, her clothes wrinkled, making her way to the table.

"Hello. How are you feeling?" Maka asked.

"Tired."

"Would you like a cup of tea or something to eat?" Alan asked.

"Tea. Please."

Alan went to the kitchen to make her some tea.

"You should eat something."

"Later."

Trying to break the silence Alan noticed a deck of cards and a couple of board games.

"Why don't we play some cards or one of these games?"

The girls looked over at the stack of games.

"Or how about a movie?" Maka chimed in.

"OK." Aiyana could hardly hold her head up she was so exhausted and drained.

Maka saw a little disappointed look on Alan's face. "Maybe we can watch one of your movies, Alan."

Alan grinned. "Maybe."

Akéšaglogaŋ

18

The living room was dark, and the screen saver on the television rolled the display images. Maka and Aiyana were lying asleep on opposite ends of the couch, Alan fast asleep in the reclining chair when the phone rang.

Maka jumped quickly, her phone next to her. She answered it quietly trying not to wake anyone and left the room. Whispering "Hello," she looked at the clock, 4:44 a.m.

It was McKenzie. "We have a plane waiting for you. You need to get back to the Res. We have information on Hurd."

"When is the car coming to get me?"

"Should be in the driveway now. See you soon."

Maka hung up the phone and grabbed her bag, putting a few things in it. She quickly splashed some cold water on her face, brushed her teeth, and pulled her hair back in a ponytail. Grabbing a small towel, a little soap and water, did a quick French bath. She grabbed her things and started down the hallway running into Alan.

"Good morning," Alan said, in his cute morning voice, still a little groggy just waking up.

"Good morning." She hugged him and kissed him on the cheek.

"Are we leaving?"

Pulling Alan into the bedroom, she said, "I have to go, but you and Aiyana will stay here until I come back."

"We should go with you."

"No, safer here."

"How long will you be gone? Where are you going?"

"I have to go back to the Res. I'm not sure, maybe a day or two. You guys will be safer here. I need to know you both are safe."

"But…"

"Alan, I will do my job better knowing you are here. Please."

Alan gently brought her to him.

"I will be worried; how will I know if you are safe?"

"We will stay in touch. I have to leave. They are waiting for me outside."

Alan didn't want to let her go, he wanted to pull her closer to him, protect her. Here she was protecting him. She started to try and pull back. He slowly lifted his embrace, leaning down he softly pressed his lips against her, their breath becoming one. Maka broke the kiss.

"I'm sorry. I have to go. I will call you and text you. Please take care of Aiyana until I get back."

"Of course. I will look out for her."

Maka went to pick up her bag, Alan grabbed it and walked her to the front door. Aiyana was still asleep on the couch. Maka took her bag and kissed him on the cheek as she walked out the door.

"Lock this behind me."

Alan closed the door, locking it slowly. He walked over to the CCTV and watched Maka get into a black SUV. He took a step back and investigated the living room. Aiyana was still fast asleep. He couldn't help but think to himself, *What am I going to do with a teenager, in this house?*

He decided to make coffee and call Jerry, even though Maka instructed him not to have contact with anyone.

***

The black SUV pulled up to the hangar of the private jet that was waiting for Maka. She jumped out quickly and was greeted at the stairs by the pilot. "Agent Mahpiya?"

"Yes." Maka showed him her credentials.

"Nice to meet you. We will be taking off as soon as you are on board."

She walked up the stairs followed by the pilot.

"How long is the flight?"

"About two and a half hours."

Maka looked at her watch, 6:03 am.

Alan was in his room, door closed, lying in bed with his laptop in his lap. He was dialing Jerry's number.

"Alan where the hell are you!"

"Good morning to you, Jer."

"Well!"

"I'm not exactly sure. You wouldn't believe me if I told you. I hardly believe it myself."

"The pages you sent only satisfied the studio for a minute. You know that you need to send more."

"Tell them they will get the rest when it's done. I'm not sending anything more."

"*Where are you?*"

"I'm not exactly sure. You cannot tell anyone we had this conversation. We are in a safe house."

"A *what?*"

"You heard me. They are keeping us here until they say it's safe for me to come home."

"Who the hell are they? What happened? How? When will they know it's safe?"

"I just wanted to call and tell you I am working on the screenplay, and I will have it finished."

"You can't leave me hanging like this. What happened?"

"All I can say right now is what a story! There is a movie here."

"You're not going to tell me, are you?"

"No. I have to go. They told me not to have any contact with anyone. I just wanted to let you know. I will call you as soon as I know more. Bye, Jer."

"Be safe."

Alan hung up. He checked his messages, but nothing from Maka. He decided he'd better work on the screenplay while Aiyana was still asleep.

***

9:29a.m. Wheels down. Maka's plane arrived at Chardon airport. She recognized it immediately looking out the window. She forgot about the time change; Pine Ridge was an hour ahead of San Diego. She wondered how Alan and Aiyana were getting along. As they taxied down the runway, Maka could see McKenzie standing next to an SUV. She quickly sent Alan a message. "How are you? Is Aiyana feeling better?" Almost immediately she received a response from Alan. "OK. Wish you were here. She is still asleep."

Maka responded "We landed. I will call you tonight."

Maka put her phone away, grabbed her bag, and headed toward the door.

McKenzie approached Maka as she exited the plane and began debriefing her immediately as they walked toward the SUV.

"He returned around one o'clock this morning. The agents have him and his guys under surveillance. The SOG (Special Operations Group) is at the hotel getting ready, we will meet them there."

They got into the back of the vehicle being driven by Agent Carrol.

"Did you hear?"

"What?"

"They are thinking about calling this off."

"What. Why!"

"The higher powers that be, don't believe that your findings are accurate."

"That doesn't surprise me, they don't want to believe there is corruption in the law enforcement department. What about that police department in Oklahoma? Half of the officers walked out because of corruption in the department."

Maka shifted around in the vehicle.

"Let's go get the son of bitch."

Akénapčiyuŋka

19

An unsuspecting Hurd paced in his living room, the heels of his boots echoing on the wood floors. The room was decorated in Native American décor, a brown stressed leather couch, and buffalo skin hide hung on the wall. A handsome headdress made of the most beautiful feathers, a detailed leather band, and medicine colors were placed in a special place in the room encased behind glass.

Two men stood near the door, armed, shoulder holsters with 9mms. Hurd was on the phone. "What the hell were you thinking? I told you to get rid of those girls after the brother showed up!"

Unbeknown to them, Hurd's house was also under surveillance by the cartel.

McKenzie and Maka pulled up to a nondescript building. Inside were the other agents.

They strode down the hallway to the main conference room, where assignments were handed out and they could be debriefed on the situation. The agents sat at a long, highly glossed wooden table. On one wall was an oversize U.S. Marshal's logo, and opposite that was the American flag. A large, digital flat screen was mounted on the far side of the room, and a tablet lay at the head of the table.

The forensic team used a dirt box to pinpoint Hurd's location. They debriefed Maka as to the plan to take Hurd into custody. As they went over the plan with them, the women put on their bullet resistant vests and tactical gear.

Agent Bynes explained the situation. "What we know is Hurd is in his home, he has his men posted around the property. There are two men in the home with him. On the exterior, three men are surrounding the home rotating in different positions, at different times."

"Once we arrive, we have one shot to take him into custody." McKenzie chimed in.

***

Alan walked into the kitchen with his empty coffee cup in one hand, and laptop in the other, looking comfortable wearing sweatpants and a t-shirt supplied to them from the airport gift shop. He was slightly startled when he turned the corner, not expecting to see Aiyana standing against the counter eating a bowl of cereal. He noticed the clock on the microwave read 11:11 am.

"Good morning, I didn't see you at first. Did you sleep well?" Alan walked over to pour a cup of coffee.

"Think so."

"Then you slept well," Alan said with a smile.

"I suppose. Where's Maka?"

"She had to leave very early this morning for work. She didn't want to wake you. But she'll call us tonight."

"When will she be back?"

"She just said soon."

"So, we are stuck here? Why can't we leave?"

Alan walked over and sat down at the high-top counter. "She told me she needed us to stay so she could do her job better knowing we are safe."

"This is so unfair."

Aiyana tossed her bowl in the sink and walked back to the living room, flopping on the couch. She pulled up a blanket, curling up under it, she started scrolling through the television for something to watch.

***

Hurd was talking to the men in the room with him when another man joined them. Dressed in coveralls, hair in a pigtail. It was the yardman. Hurd yelled at the top of his lungs.

"Well, it's about time! I need you to go back to the hotel and get rid of everything! I mean it, do it now!"

The yardman stared at him for a moment. "What would you like me to do with it?"

"I don't care, just get rid of everything. Someplace it can't be found."

He turned and left as Hurd answered his phone. "Get your ass over here now!"

Maka and her team were at the end of the road just less than a mile from Hurd's. They waited for the call from the agents surveilling the house to move in. Hidden off in the distance just on the other side of the hill, the cartel men watched as the U.S. Marshals began to make their move onto Hurd's house.

The call came in, "A male just left Hurd's."

Maka was concerned it was Hurd. "Who was it?"

"We don't have a positive identity on the man. Appears in his forty's, tall, wearing coveralls."

"Have one of your guys follow him. We are on our way to you."

Maka hung up, "Let's go!"

The team formed a convoy of four SUVs, driving at high speed to meet up with the first team who were in view of Hurd's house. They had enough manpower in the area to handle the raid. If Hurd decided to run, they had him covered.

They rolled up to the six agents on the scene, four men and two women standing around two government-issued vehicles, dressed in their tactical gear, making final weapon checks. The agents knew their assignment and were getting into position.

The lead SUV of the convoy pulled up to the agents, rolling down the passenger side window, it was Maka.

"Hey, are you ready?"

"Yes ma'am! Only a couple hundred yards ahead around those trees."

"Let's do a quick radio check, everyone has their earpieces in?"

All the agents went one by one checking they had a connection.

All clear, all the agents wore body armor, some agents had ballistic helmets on, while others pulled down their black balaclavas and got into their vehicles. They sped off quickly, Maka's vehicle was the third to go.

A cloud of dust hid most of the vehicles as they came speeding up to Hurd's gate, the dash lights could barely be seen. The gate was closed. The lead truck used its ram to break open the gate. Hurd's security opened fire on the trucks as they sped past. The last SUV stopped, and two agents jumped out, taking down the gunman, and securing him as the others raced toward the front of the home.

Each vehicle approached the front yard of the house, the lead truck digging its tires into the lawn. Agents took strategic positions. Their faces were covered, and their sunglasses reflected the afternoon sun, firearms in hand, wearing their raid jackets, and vests identifying them as U.S. MARSHAL FUGITIVE TASK FORCE or just U.S. MARSHAL. They rushed the house from all sides yelling out "MARSHAL – DROP YOUR WEAPON - GET DOWN ON THE GROUND!"

Shots were fired from inside the residence at the agents. The agents returned fire, killing one person inside. The gunfire ended, and one agent was grazed by a bullet to his shoulder, his ballistic vest prevented any further injuries. Agents deployed flash bangs, one in the front entryway and one in the backyard, but no one exited the house. They entered to clear the six-bedroom house, Hurd's men surrendering as they entered the living room.

Hurd was in the far rear of the house; he heard the flash bang and gunfire. He yelled at one of his men. "Don't just stand there!" The man ran out of the room, while the other man tried to reach the rest of the security team on his radio, but no one answered him.

"Cartel."

Hurd went to his gun cabinet and took out a Remington Fieldmaster 870 pump action shotgun and a Barrett M82 semi-automatic rifle. "Put that away, use this," handing the M82 to the man.

Hurd took out a Koch HK45 and two extra mags that he put in his back pocket.

There were two doors leading to the room they were in, a large picture window with the blinds closed, one wall lined with bookshelves, and the other wall decorated with pictures and awards.

"Go out this door." The man took point. He led Hurd out of the room, and down a hallway. They could hear faint yelling coming from the front of the house. They walked cautiously, not knowing from which direction they could be ambushed.

The agents had secured the house and had it surrounded. As the agents handcuffed and contained the security team, Maka found herself alone. "I'll be right behind you," McKenzie assured Maka. Her heart was racing, adrenaline pumping through her veins so much she began to feel superhuman. All her senses were heightened, and she had one thing on her mind, getting Hurd.

She continued through the house making her way to the last room Hurd was in. She saw the other door and moved towards it speaking into her headset, "Watch the rear, he is headed toward the back of the house." She continued slowly down the hallway, it was darker than other parts of the house, there were no windows, and it felt like it would never end. There was a creak in the floorboards behind her. Stopping and swinging her firearm around, it was McKenzie. "Whoa. It's me. Didn't you hear me on the radio?"

"No! Come on." They came to two closed doors, and they found themselves in a flanking position. Maka pulled out her flashlight. They prepared to open the door, using hand motions to cue each other, counting down by the show of fingers-three, two, one. Maka, having to use a flashlight, threw open the door and McKenzie cleared the room. Back in the hallway, they continued to the second door. Same procedure, the door flew open, and they found it led to stairs going up to the attic.

Maka felt they should continue down the hallway, there was some light toward the end of it. She motioned to McKenzie to follow. As they came into the light, it opened to a large kitchen where she saw a shadow across the floor. Motioning to McKenzie to the position taking a deep breath, the agents gripped their firearms tighter. Maka made the first move, "MARSHAL GET DOWN ON THE GROUND!" She looked and could see the man pointing the rifle at her. "DROP YOUR WEAPON," he didn't. She repeated herself, again and again. She heard a click, which in a millisecond, indicated to her he was about to fire, she fired at the same time, hitting the man.

McKenzie was checking the man down, using plastic ties to secure his hands. Hurd came from around the corner, getting ready to take the shot. Maka saw Hurd. She fired her weapon, hitting him in the arm. He dropped his gun immediately, she charged him "DOWN ON THE GROUND NOW HANDS WHERE I CAN SEE THEM! DOWN NOW!" Hurd had no other choice but to concede, they had him covered. He smirked at her, as he lowered himself slowly to his knees, his eyes piercing through her soul. She knew she had him. He knew he had her.

***

The house was dark inside, the television light illuminated the living room, spilling slightly into the kitchen. Alan came out of his room, he was very proud of himself, he was in the final stretch of his screenplay's first draft. He was walking toward the kitchen and realized Aiyana had been watching television all day. It seemed she hadn't left the couch at all.

"Hi, have you eaten anything?" Alan gently approached her.

"No."

"Would you like me to make you something?"

"No."

"Can I do anything for you?" Alan sat on the recliner chair and tried to talk with her.

She ignored his last question. Still feeling the effects of the drugs lingering in her system, she was depleted.

She shook her head no.

Alan rummaged through the cupboards and found a bag of popcorn kernels. He decided to make some and put the dominoes on the table. He'd hoped the aroma from the fresh popcorn would lure Aiyana into the kitchen.

"Aiyana, can you please come into the kitchen."

A few minutes had passed, and Alan was drizzling melted butter on the popcorn when Aiyana stepped into the room.

"Hey there kiddo, how about some popcorn and dominos?"

She looked at him as if he had three heads. She never had an adult offer a game night before, not like this. She shrugged her shoulders and walked over to the table, pushed around a couple of dominoes and flopped on the chair, brought up her legs, wrapping her arms around her knees. She appeared cold, guarded. Alan grabbed a couple of sodas and brought everything to the table.

"Did you get to rest today?"

"Yeah."

"Have you ever played dominoes before?"

"Once. I kinda remember."

Alan started to set up the game, laying out the dominos. Aiyana just stared, wondering what he wanted from her. She never experienced any man, much less a white man, who was kind and just wanted to play an innocent game.

Alan appeared excited, he was getting cabin fever and needed a distraction from being locked in the house for over twenty-four hours now. He opened his Coke, grabbed a handful of popcorn, and looked over at Aiyana smiling like a little boy.

"OK, ladies first."

The look of surprise on her face told Alan a lot. She placed her domino.

"You want to play dominos," she said trying to hold back a smile, as the corners of her mouth couldn't help but slide up.

"Yes. I don't know about you; this house is starting to feel a little claustrophobic."

"I hadn't noticed."

Aiyana reached for the popcorn; Alan was glad to see her eat some.

"Can I ask what you were working on today?

"A screenplay. I finished the draft and sent it off to my agent earlier. Waiting for notes."

"What is it about?"

"Probably no one you would know. An old Hollywood actress, about her life."

Aiyana was beating Alan in their first round of the game.

"Are you sure you only played this once?" Alan snickered.

"Yes. I'm sure." She said with a little grin.

They continued to play in comfortable silence, occasionally breaking it with a light conversation about the game. Alan wanted to keep it that way, just to have a little fun.

***

On the Reservation, the operation was not over yet. Agents cleared several vehicles that were in the driveway. They broke the windows on some because the tint was too dark to see if anyone was hiding inside. The vehicles included a black Escalade, a Cadillac XT6, a Maserati, and a Dually Dodge Ram pickup. The team was rounding up Hurd and all his men when two tribal police officers showed up. "What the hell is going on here? You can't do this! You're way out of your jurisdiction."

Maka got a call from the agents who followed the yardman.

"Mahpiya."

"Go ahead," Maka responded.

"You're not going to believe this. We followed the suspect to what appeared to be a hotel on the Res, not far from the man camps."

"I know the one."

"Well, appears there are at least a couple of girls here, he is getting ready to move."

Maka looked over to McKenzie and another agent and waived them over.

"How do you want to proceed?" Bynes asked for clarification.

"We are on our way, don't let him out of your sight. If he makes any moves stop him."

Maka motioned to the agents to get into one of the SUVs. Passing one of the lead agents she informed him briefly.

"Bynes found girls at the hotel."

The agent nodded "Get out of here, we got this."

Maka jumped into the driver's seat and sped off kicking up so much dust you couldn't see the road any longer.

The agent addressed the Tribal Officers, assuring them they were in their jurisdiction and pulled them aside to debrief them. The officers fought the agent, trying to convince them they had to turn Hurd over to them. The agents refused and told them to take it up with their director. They continued to load the suspects into their vehicles. The reservation had a history of corruption amongst their own law enforcement, especially working with the pipeline companies. The agents were aware of this, trying their best to escort the Chief from the reservation as fast as they could.

Maka reached Bynes, his position was covered by the trees near the river, out of sight of the yardman but in clear line of sight of the hotel.

"What is he doing?"

"He put the girls in the back of that white worker truck, the one without the windows. He went over to that barn with two full black garbage bags, they appeared heavy, he dragged them most of the way. He just went back inside. Oh, wait…"

The man exited the building dragging another large black bag.

"Let's go." The three agents jumped in their vehicles and drove the grooves made by the previous vehicles. The yardman was coming out of the barn about 100 yards from the van he put the girls in. He saw the SUVs coming towards him, he tried to run for the van, Maka and Bynes made it to the van first and blocked it in. McKenzie jumped out, gun raised and pointed at him.

"GET DOWN ON THE GROUND NOW!"

Maka and Bynes cautiously approach the van, firearms drawn. "Cover me," Maka slowly reached for the door, she opened it quickly and stepped back prepared to fire. Two girls cowered in the back. Bynes cleared the van, he looked over to check on McKenzie, she was struggling to get the man to comply with her demands.

"I got McKenzie, you check the girls."

Maka entered the van, and he backed up McKenzie. The yardman continued to walk away from her. "STOP U.S. MARSHAL!" He had one hand near his waistband, he stopped and drew his weapon as he turned quickly. Bynes was just approaching McKenzie, "GUN!" he yelled. He immediately took the shot, the yardman returning fire, rounds were going off so fast you couldn't tell where they were coming from. The yardman was hit multiple times, fell to his knees, and raised his gun to his head.

"NO! DON'T!" McKenzie yelled running towards him, as he pulled the trigger.

The gun gave off a 'click' sound, he was out of bullets. McKenzie approached cautiously; the yardman pointed the gun at her. "Kill me," he said in a panic, his wounds bleeding through his clothing, he fell forward, weakening from his wounds.

"Put your hands where I can see them."

"I didn't want to do it. They made me!" He repeated it several times. He yelled out and began to cry. McKenzie cuffed him. "What do you mean they made you?

"They threatened to kill my family."

McKenzie finished securing his hands and took the gun away.

"Kill me. If you don't kill me, they will and they won't be nice about it.

McKenzie looked for Bynes, he was bent over a few feet behind her. She kept her gun pointed at the yardman.

"Hey, hey, are you OK?"

He tried to stand up straight and downplay the pain he was in. "Yeah, sure. Just got nicked."

"You're shot!"

"Just a scratch." He walked closer to her and on his way fell to a knee. She left the yardman handcuffed and wounded. She ran over to Bynes, looking him over she could see the bullet somehow clipped the edge of his armor, he had been hit multiple times. She helped him loosen the vest, "Looks like one went through your abdomen." As they took off his vest, they could see he was bleeding.

"That's going to bruise." He tried to make a joke.

"Let's get you to the truck." She helped him up and laid him on the back seat of their SUV. She left the man in the field and called for medical assistance, "Send the helicopter, agent down," she demanded.

Maka came around the outside of the van. "The girls are coming out of whatever he gave them. They need medical attention."

"Was Dakota…?"

"No."

Wikčémna Núnpa

20

The sun was starting to go down, a black SUV turned down Kansas City Street, big letters on the side of the red brick building: 'PUBLIC SAFETY BUILDING, RAPID CITY POLICE DEPARTMENT PENNINGTON COUNTY SHERIFF DEPARTMENT.' A news van with KOTA NEWS shrink wrapped around it parked across the street, a cameraman and reporter scrambling to set up to go live. The black SUV pulled into a reserved parking spot. Two men came out of the vehicle, wearing black golf shirts, jeans, and boots. They walked into the building, stopped at the front desk, and showed their credentials. The desk sergeant buzzed the door for them to enter immediately. The hallway buzzed with federal agents from three different agencies, Marshals, Sheriff, Rapid City PD, as well as the Tribal Investigator.

"Where's Agent Mahpiya?" one of the men asked the Sheriff.

"She is in Interview Room B."

"Get her out of there and get me an office." He demanded.

Hurd was handcuffed to a table, Maka sat across from him. They stared at each other in silence for minutes that seemed like hours. She started to interview Hurd before anyone else got to him. She was determined to learn more about his operation and find the whereabouts of Dakota, knowing if another agency questioned him first, she may never get an answer.

The sheriff's deputy knocked on the interview room door. She ignored the knocks, continuing to repeat her questions to Hurd, he refused to answer her questions or react to her threatening demands.

"My arm is killing me; I need to be in the hospital."

"It's a scratch, you are not going anywhere until you tell me where Dakota is."

There was another knock on the door. Frustrated, Maka got up abruptly and stepped outside the room into the hallway. The door closed behind her, "There is an agent from the FBI here, who wants to talk to you, he is waiting in the office."

Maka couldn't believe it, she shook her head and started to make her way to the office.

"Wait here please. Don't let anyone in or out. I will be right back."

"Sure." The sheriff stood outside the door.

She made her way to the other office. Standing in front of the office door, she took a deep breath before she knocked.

"Come in."

She walked into the room; the agent was standing by the window looking out.

"Mahpiya, what the hell do you think you are doing?"

She recognized him immediately, Executive Assistant Director Walker of the New York office of the FBI. They worked together in the past before she left the bureau for the Marshals.

"Sir?" she was stunned. "Doing my job."

He turned and looked her sternly in the eye.

"You are done. I will take it from here. Director wants you in his office tomorrow."

"Sir, I don't understand. We are still missing a girl, and…" she stopped herself.

"No one talks to him until I am done. Got it?"

Walker starts waving a piece of paper at her and then reads off a list.

"And these charges—aggravated promotion of prostitution, kidnap, engaging in criminal activity, money laundering, tampering with evidence and compelling prostitution by force, threat, or fraud—and it keeps going Mahpiya!"

"How were you able to get the judge to hold Hurd with a $1.5 million bond?"

"I didn't."

"Who did?"

"I am not sure. I was just as surprised as you."

"Your itinerary has been sent. You fly out first thing in the morning. It is all in your email."

"I need to speak with the Director, this is my case."

"I will be taking care of the interviewing. The DOJ (Department of Justice) will be contacting you. That's all. Take McKenzie with you."

He picked up his briefcase and walked past Maka. Stopping before he walked out of the room, he looked at her.

"Should have stayed with the bureau." He smirked and walked out.

She was confused, this was not normal protocol, leaving the office infuriated. McKenzie saw her walk by and could tell she was seething. Maka grabbed her bag and stormed out. McKenzie was trying to keep up, walking behind her. She finally caught up to her as they exited the building. "Maka, what happened? Would you stop?"

"That asshole! He took me off my case. How can he do that? He can't do that, right?" She continued to ramble on. McKenzie let her vent.

"I mean, it's my case damn it! Something isn't right. I need to call the Director." She walked to the SUV and threw her bag inside, started going through her pockets to look for her phone. McKenzie saw she tossed the phone with the bag and leaned in, handing Maka the phone.

"I just saw we have orders to be on a red-eye tonight and in the office first thing in the morning."

"Damn it, just goes to his voicemail. I'm messaging him."

"Get in the truck, I'll drive. We need to get packed and head to the airport, it's getting late."

They had a long drive to go back and get their things from the hotel and turn around to be back at the airport in time for their flight. It was almost as if it were planned this way to remove them from any further involvement in the case.

McKenzie was silent for the most part, giving Maka some time to cool down.

"Who knows about the safe house?" Maka was staring out the window lost in thought. She started to wonder if Alan and Aiyana were safe.

"Well, us and Reed. The Director. I don't think he informed anyone else of the identity of who is there."

"Something feels off. I need to get them out of there."

"I'm sure they are fine. Reed would never let anything happen to them. He is a boy scout through and through. You know that."

"Maybe so."

Maka messaged Alan. *"Hi, how are you two doing?"* She didn't want to alarm him of anything.

Then she messaged Reed. *"Hi. How are things going over there?"* She waited for their response. It took an unusually long time for Reed to respond.

"All clear here. Quiet. How did it go on your end?"

"Subjects in custody."

"Whoop! Whoop! Can't wait to hear all about it. Nice job!"

"Reed please let me know if anything changes or if you hear anything from HQ."

"Good. Copy."

Maka was surprised she hadn't heard back from Alan yet. She messaged him again.

"Hello?"

McKenzie pulled into the hotel where they were staying. "Let's grab our stuff and get to the airport. This is taking longer than I thought."

Maka received a message from Alan.

"Hi. How are you? Miss you. We are good. Hung out and played some games. When are you coming back?"

Maka was relieved. Things sounded fine.

"Hi. I'm glad you guys are doing well. I should be back in a couple of days. I will call you later. We are on our way to the airport."

She was about to set her phone down, hesitating. She was nervous to be vulnerable with him, but at the same time, she felt silly for feeling that way. There was something about him that put her spirit at ease. She messaged him, *"Miss you too."* She and McKenzie met up in the hallway.

"All set. Let's go... Did you get ahold of Alan?

"Yes. Sounds like things are OK."

"Good."

They got back in the SUV and headed for the airport.

"Did you look over the itinerary?" Maka was scrolling through her emails looking them over.

"Yes, I'm not sure why either of us has to go to Virginia. Why can't we debrief here?"

"It has to be because of Hurd's involvement."

"Could be."

"What time are you scheduled?" Maka asked.

"Not until 2:30 pm. You?"

"9 am. Weird. We should be going together."

They found their government-issued plane waiting for them. There were three male agents already on board dressed in t-shirts and jeans, all sitting in seats with their laptops open. None of them looked familiar to the women. The men greeted the ladies with a nod, no words exchanged. It was late and all Maka could think about was Alan and Aiyana.

Wikčémna Waŋží

21

Morning came quick, Maka had been summoned to the field office for an interview with a group of federal agents and the Director. It was fairly routine, headquarters was always dispatching inspection teams to make sure agents were doing their job.

She pulled her government-issued Jeep Liberty up to the security gate and flashed her credentials at the guard, who waved her through. The parking garage was nearly empty. *That's odd,* she thought.

A couple of agents stood by the entrance. Maka chatted with them briefly. In the past, they seemed standoffish, but today they seemed unusually friendly. She mentioned her meeting.

"Good luck," one of them said. The encounter left her with an uneasy feeling.

Maka arrived on the eighth floor and checked in. She was instructed to use the office down the hall to prepare for her meeting.

Sitting down at the desk she started to replay certain moments. That at 9:30 in the morning, the eighth floor was empty, usually around 9:45 am a few people trickled in. As she was sitting in the room, an agent she had only seen maybe twice in her life walked past her open door, appearing to glance into the room.

After Maka checked her email and reviewed her files, the inspector happened to enter the room. He offered to take her upstairs for the interview, which felt off.

They rode the elevator to the eleventh floor in silence. The interview room was down the hall. Fighting her growing sense of dread, two F.B.I. SWAT team members appeared.

"Agent Mahpiya, we need you to surrender your weapon, two fingers."

Maka stopped and thought, *Here we go.* She pulled open her jacket and with two fingers lift her service-issued Glock. The SWAT officer took it from her, and the other officer reached for her magazine, removing it.

"Your badge."

She was shocked, handing over her credentials to him.

"Follow me."

One officer walked ahead while the other walked behind Maka, they led her into a small room. Well, game time, she thought. It's shocking when you want to be rescuing people, kicking in doors, executing search warrants, and saving the day and then you get blocked.

It's all cloak and dagger that is a disaffecting experience. You get agents who try hard and hit that point where they just can't do it anymore and burn out. She could be working the case instead of being called for interrogation.

Three agents, a woman and two men, sat at the table with an open laptop with photos of her in Tijuana with Daddy, and documents spread out across the table. The woman spoke first, "Have a seat. Tell me about these," she said.

"I don't know what that is. I have never seen it before." Maka was confused.

"Where did you get these?" she asked.

"We are asking the questions. You were out of your jurisdiction. We can't build a case without the right supporting evidence."

The bureau believed sources could give them information over agents at times. From all the documents laid out, Maka could see they had a surveillance team on the case. Surveillance teams monitored phone calls, read through emails, and followed her.

"I thought I was having a meeting with the Director. He approved all my requests for this operation. You must have those documents."

The agent looked at the other inspectors, they sorted through their paperwork. Shaking their heads, "No. we don't."

"There were emails, look through my emails."

"Did you have any contact with the cartel?"

"Not that I am aware of, just the man in those photos, they called him Daddy. He didn't appear cartel."

"He isn't, he is part of some gang, from LA. We have intel on their operation in Atlantic City, this is the first we have seen them in Tijuana. Why were you with Chief Hurd?"

"I wasn't with him. He just showed up. I was shocked to see him there."

"What was he doing?" the Inspector went on questioning Maka as if she had something to do with Hurd and the operation.

"I don't know. He was talking to some men. He did follow us to our car and his men followed us to the border. At least, it appeared to be his men at the time."

"You cannot confirm?"

"Well, yes, no…I saw one of the men that followed us was with Hurd."

"Did you see Hurd with any of the girls?"

"No, I did not."

"Did either of your witnesses?"

"I have not been able to take their full statements yet. I'm here instead."

Maka was getting frustrated. She knew some of what they saw, but wasn't ready to report on it, not yet. She felt as if they were accusing her of wrongdoing. She also knew this was part of the politics, the game. When someone is under suspicion within the law enforcement umbrella, everyone becomes a suspect.

The male inspector spoke up, changing the subject.

"What was $5,000?"

"Mexican guards at the border wouldn't let us pass, you know how they are down there. I had to pay their agents off to get us out of there." Maka was getting impatient.

"Ask the Director if he approved all of this."

The male Inspector, whom Maka didn't recognize, spoke, but didn't make eye contact, he looked down at the file in front of him almost the entire time.

"During the raid, who shot Hurd?"

"I did. He was getting ready to fire at Agent McKenzie."

"Where is the safe house?"

Maka looked at him and the other inspectors. She thought that was a strange question, the other inspectors seemed to think so as well. One even murmured, "That is irrelevant for this meeting."

Maka didn't answer, she looked at the female inspector, who pulled out a document and slid it in front of Maka.

"This was a request you made, and it was declined. But you went to California anyway. Who approved you to go there to further the investigation?"

"At first no one, I was on personal time. I attended Paythan's funeral and chatted with some of the people there. It led me to find out more information about the case and I decided to share it with the Deputy and Director to further the investigation. They approved it at that point."

"Who approved it? I don't see anything documented. I do see a request to further investigations and Hurd is mentioned."

"Yes, ma'am. I believe he knows what happened to the girls."

"Were you aware of the investigation of upward of 300 women in his trafficking? The ring also operated out of houses in San Diego."

"No. I was not."

"Your little escapade almost blew months of surveillance and thousands of dollars on this investigation."

"If this were to get out about a Native American Police Chief, you do know what the media will do?"

There was a knock at the door, a woman stepped in and motioned to the inspectors to follow her.

"Wait here." The female inspector looked at Maka as she gathered her files. The other inspectors took their files and closed the laptop. Maka sat back, letting out a deep breath. She knew there would be recording devices in the room. She sat emotionless while she waited. She replayed the questioning over and over in her head. It suddenly hit her, there must be another case going on that she stumbled in the middle of, but why wouldn't they share that with her? They did say they had been investigating the rappers.

What seemed like hours was about ten minutes when the female inspector returned to the room.

"Interview is over. You have someone looking over you. You will be contacted by the Missing Child Unit about the girl." She turned to walk back out of the room.

"Aiyana," Maka spoke up. It struck a chord with her that the inspector was so cold and disrespectful.

"What?"

"The girl. Her name is Aiyana."

"Right." With one hand on the door about to open it, the inspector stopped and held the door closed.

"Ma'am, can I return to my witnesses?"

"Yes, I suggest that be the first place you go when you leave here, take your statements from them and submit your report."

She opened the door "You can get your things from Agent Brown on eight. The Director will be in touch." She walked out, letting the door close behind her.

Maka sat in her car in the parking garage, gathering herself. She tried to call McKenzie but had no service. She thought she better let her know what happened. As she got on the highway, her phone had service again and it was blowing up with messages, texts, voicemails, and emails.

She dialed McKenzie, and it rang and went to voicemail. "Call me as soon as you get this, it's important."

She called Reed, which went to voicemail, she left him a message "Call me, I'm texting you too."

Texting Reed to call her, she texted Alan to call her as well. She headed to get her things, and while she was driving, she made arrangements for a flight to San Diego.

Something was feeling off, she knew she uncovered an operation much bigger than she anticipated. She could just feel with everything in her that something was wrong. Thinking to herself, Hurd pissed off the cartel, skinheads, that LA gang and there is corruption within a law enforcement agency. Now with Paythan gone, the key witnesses were Alan, Aiyana, and herself. Talking to herself, *Okay I need to breathe.* Her phone was ringing, which startled her. "McKenzie!"

"Maka are you OK? How did the interview go?"

"Yes, I think. It was more like an interrogation."

"They canceled mine. Told me to go back to Pennington."

"What? What the hell."

"Where are you?"

"On my way back to San Diego."

"I wonder why they didn't send us together."

"What did I do wrong?"

"What do you mean?"

"Everything. I was idealistic when I joined the Marshals." Maka went on to say "I wanted to make a difference in both worlds, my people, and bridge the rest of the world. I believe I could help make things better, which may sound naïve. The war on trafficking is like a game, right? It's a very dangerous and toxic environment, and maybe we screwed up here, what we are doing is wrong. Hiding that one of our own is capable of being one of the monsters behind it all."

"Maka, breathe. Can you tell me what happened this morning?"

Reed was calling in. "I'll call you back, I have to take this."

"Reed, where have you been? Are they OK?"

"Hi. Yes, we are all OK. I was just having coffee with Alan. Interesting guy, ya know he is like a big-time Hollywood writer. He knows the coolest celebrities."

"Yes, I know." She was frustrated. Have you heard from anyone? Anyone from the team or the Director?"

"You know he would never call me. Deputy Marshal Walters did call this morning. He wanted a status report, and said they were sending someone to relieve me."

"I'm on my way to the airport, taking the next flight out. I should be there in six hours or so. Reed, something is off, promise me you won't leave them until I get there."

"You got it." He disconnected the call.

Anxious to get back to Alan, she pressed the accelerator until it hit the floor, she turned on her dash lights and siren.

Wikčémna Núnpa Núnpa

22

The house was dark, it was after midnight. Maka cautiously drove up the driveway with her headlights off. She passed Reed's car, he waved her in. She parked outside the garage letting herself in through the backdoor. The only light on was in the kitchen over the sink, she didn't want to wake anyone. As she passed the living room, she noticed the TV on, and Aiyana asleep on the couch. Alan was asleep in his room. She quietly made her way to her room, and immediately stepped into the shower.

Towel-drying her hair, she caught her reflection in the mirror, she was wearing a white tank see-through and very short boxers. She looked herself in the eyes, thinking about the first night she and Alan kissed. She shook her head, then found herself slowly making her way into his room to his bed. She paused, watching him sleep for a moment, slowly pulling back the sheet, he was shirtless, wearing sweatpants. She slid her way under the covers and gently glided her arm across the hairs of his chest, her hand gently cupping the side of his face, waking him. He was slightly startled but quickly was pleasantly surprised, still half asleep she whispered in his ear, "Hi."

He turned toward her, his nose brushing hers, "Hi." She kissed him, he reciprocated slowly, softly.

Morning came, and Maka was up before Alan. She slipped out of bed almost as gracefully as she slipped in. She got dressed as she closed the door behind her and turned to go back to her room, she ran into Aiyana coming out of the bathroom. She looked at Maka, and grinned, "You're back." Maka was a bit embarrassed, quickly diverting the situation, "Hungry? Let me make you something." She walked past Aiyana, stopping at her room and grabbing a sweatshirt.

Maka and Aiyana were chatting in the kitchen as they made breakfast together, Alan watched, admiring the connection, the girls seemed to be sharing. Maka saw him out of the corner of her eye, "Good morning."

"Good morning, ladies." He walked closer.

"Coffee?"

"Please."

Aiyana poured him a cup and slid it to him on the counter.

"Sit, we're making breakfast for you." She smiled.

Alan sat sipping his coffee enjoying the view, from an outside perspective it looked like a happy family.

"So, did you finish your screenplay?"

Alan sat straight up.

"I did. Thank you for asking. Submitted it and now I wait."

"Congratulations!"

"Are you going to tell us what happened? Did you find him?" Alan sipped his coffee.

Maka and Aiyana brought food to the table.

"We did. Hurd is in custody. We are tying a few loose ends and you should be able to go home any day now."

Aiyana played with her food, her face now showing disappointment. She began to worry about what would happen to her, and where she would go. Maka and Alan saw the sudden energy change in her and quickly looked at one another.

"Aiyana, you will be OK. I will make sure of it."

Maka wanted to hug her and tell her everything would be OK, but she didn't want to overstep. This was one of those moments that seemed blurred, having human compassion, or professionalism. She knew she couldn't get emotionally attached. Reflecting quickly on what she had been through, she reached for her forearm to reassure her she was there for her. Her phone rang, breaking the silence. Maka jumped to answer it.

"This is Maka."

She left the room. There was a knock at the door, Alan checked the CCTV monitor. It was Reed, he went to open the door for him.

"Where's Maka?" Reed asked.

"On the phone."

"I'll wait here."

"Come in, have a cup of coffee."

"No thank you."

Alan thought that was weird, they seemed to bond the other day and while Maka was gone Reed came in every morning for a cup of coffee. Now Reed was all business.

Maka returned to the kitchen, she looked concerned. She saw Reed. "Step outside?"

"Yes."

Alan noticed Maka was now dressed, he wondered what happened.

"Did they call you?" Reed asked.

"I just got off the phone with McKenzie. He's dead."

"Hurd?"

"That's what she said, the deputies were transporting him to a new facility, and they were ambushed. Hurd and one deputy didn't make it, the other is in a coma."

"Holy shit! Cartel?"

"Not sure, he was involved with a few gangs on and off the Res, could have been anyone of them."

"Guess we'll never know," Reed said as he walked with Maka.

"We need to know though."

"This is a big fight, Maka. All we can do is focus on saving one at a time, we will lose ourselves if we don't."

"I know, just feel I could be doing more." Maka stopped and looked off into the distance. "Thank you for taking such good care of them. They have been through a lot."

"That's what I'm here for, and Alan said he is going to invite me to a premiere of one of his movies!"

They laughed as Maka turned to go back into the house. "I guess we should pack and be on our way. I just realized; I am going to have so much paperwork!"

"I'll hang out and leave with you."

"Come in and have some breakfast."

Reed turned around; he would never pass up a chance for a meal. "OK, you twisted my arm." Before they went in the house Reed felt he had to ask, "What will happen to Aiyana?"

"I'm not sure, she will need a lot of counseling, someplace to live."

Alan and Aiyana were watching them through the window, saw them coming back towards the house, and hurried back to the table.

"Everything OK?" Alan asked Maka.

"I have some good news. We get to leave today."

"That is good news!" Alan responded. He stood to hug Maka, and they both hesitated but he didn't care and hugged her. Aiyana sat in silence.

"I think you both should come to my house, and we can make plans from there," Alan included Aiyana.

"I have to check in with the office and find out the next steps. Let's enjoy breakfast."

Aiyana seemed to have lost her appetite for a minute.

"Aiyana, no matter what, you are safe, and I will make sure you get everything you need moving forward."

Wikčémna Núŋpa Yámni

23

The government-issued vehicle pulled in front of Alan's house. Maka was the first to step out of the driver's seat, then Alan, and Aiyana.

"It should have been about a two-hour drive, but LA traffic," Alan said.

"Is it always like that? It took us like four hours," Aiyana asked, stretching.

"Not always, well maybe a lot of the time." Alan joked.

"I don't know how you do it every day. The traffic alone would be draining."

Maka closed her door and followed Alan into the house. As he unlocked the front door, he felt a tremendous heaviness lift off of him, almost as if there had been an elephant sitting on his chest for the last couple of weeks.

"Feels good to be back," he said. "Please come in, *mi casa es su casa.* Make yourselves at home."

He tossed his bag to the side; the girls dropped their bags by the front door.

"I would offer you something to drink, but we've been gone so long." He pulled out a half gallon of two percent milk, smelled it, and immediately emptied it into the garbage disposal.

Aiyana started to walk toward the back of the house and looked out the back door. There was a huge tree that looked like it had been there for hundreds of years. It was so big, and everything was so green, with beautiful flowers, lemon, and orange trees, and a pool with a waterfall. It was like being at a resort she thought to herself.

"You can go out there, it's my little oasis. I forget I'm in the middle of the city back here." He opened the door for her. They all stepped outside.

"It's beautiful," Maka commented.

Alan walked over to the orange tree and picked a couple, handing them to the girls.

"You have to try one, you can't find oranges like these in any store. One of these is like drinking a glass of orange juice."

"Thanks," Aiyana said as she explored the backyard. She walked to the pool, bending over to touch the water. It felt inviting, like bath water.

"It's heated. I probably forgot to turn it off when we left."

Maka stood on the patio and just took in the tranquility of the environment. It was so peaceful and felt healing, the blue skies, it was only in the '70s, a gentle breeze. Aiyana wandered around the yard. Alan was checking his fruit trees and Maka was just trying to be present and breathe.

Her phone went off suddenly, which made her flinch a bit. She looked. It was McKenzie.

"Hi."

"Are you still at the house?"

"No, we left a few hours ago. Why?"

"Director is looking for you. You were the last one to speak to Hurd before he died."

"I was? I thought Walker was going in after he kicked us out."

"Well, if he did, there is no record of him talking to Hurd. You're the last recorded person to have an interview."

"This is unbelievable."

"Wait, there is more."

"More?"

"Well, we are waiting for confirmation, I don't want to speak prematurely. It's not the best news."

"Tell me."

"We found two bodies."

"Bodies? Is it Dakota?"

"Deceased. We haven't identified the bodies."

"Where did they find the bodies?"

"Hurd's. A young juvenile male, and a young female."

"We went over his place with a fine-tooth comb. I don't know what to say. I need to get back there."

"Take your time, we got this. You've been through enough."

"I need to be there; I can't stay here and do nothing."

"I thought they put you on leave."

"They did, I'll see what I can do. I'll call you tomorrow."

Alan was walking toward Maka, he had the cutest smile and a little twinkle coming from his eyes. She could see he was in his element, happy to be home.

"Are you hungry?"

"Not really. You?"

"I'm getting there. I can order something, and have it delivered. Will take at least an hour by the time it would get here. Shall I order us something?"

"Sure, something simple. I'm fine with whatever you two want."

Aiyana heard the conversation. "Pizza?"

"I know the best place for pizza, come inside, I have a menu!" Alan certainly was back in his element. He went into the house to place the order. Maka stayed outside, she prayed for direction on what to do. Should she go back and help with the investigation or stay with Alan? She knew she needed to get Aiyana back to some kind of normalcy and counseling. She knew the Res didn't have the proper support Aiyana was going to need if she would ever have a chance to heal from all the traumas. She would never truly be free from the residue of all that she had been through, but she would have a better chance of rising above it with the proper counseling, medical care, support, and schooling. Maka knew she needed to help Aiyana if she was ever to have a chance to get the schooling she dreamed of.

She made a couple of calls to the Director but only got his voicemail. She called to see if she could arrange for a flight and get her leave lifted, but again voicemails. She turned and could see Aiyana helping Alan set the table. She watched for a minute, getting lost in a daydream of her possibly having a future family with him, she was dreaming of them with Aiyana laughing, enjoying dinner together, like a real family.

Alan popped his head out from inside, "Pizza will be here soon. You, OK?"

Maka snapped out of her dream, "Oh yes, couldn't be better."

She walked up to Alan and kissed him softly.

"Thank you for that," he said, holding the door open as their eyes never left each other.

Aiyana was setting the table. She was feeling relaxed, almost forgetting what she had been through for the moment. They all sat at the dinner table, Maka knew she was going to have to decide for her and Aiyana. She felt Alan would go back where he left off, but Aiyana's life had been changed forever and she had to continue working on this case.

They had fun banter over dinner, each of them exhausted, taking turns yawning.

"It's been a long day. I think we should get some rest."

Aiyana stood, picking up her plate.

"Leave them, I'll take care of it. Let me show you to your room." Alan picked up the small bag that Aiyana had and walked her to the guest room. It was bigger than any room she had ever stayed in. He walked deeper into the room and turned on the bathroom light.

"This is your bathroom, if you need anything let me know."

"Thanks." She couldn't believe she had a bathroom in the bedroom. Alan left the room, closing the door behind him. Aiyana fell backward onto the bed, talking to Paythan, "I could get used to this. Now I see why you didn't want to come back to the Res very often, Bro."

Maka stayed back and was cleaning up after dinner.

"I'll get that, please let me clean up." Alan took the plates from Maka and they cleaned them together.

"What happens to Aiyana now?" Alan asked.

"It's kinda out of my hands, DCS will be here in the morning. I did find out that because she is in child welfare and this is a federal crime, she will get a lot of help, grants to help her with medical, housing, counseling, and college."

"They will help her with school?"

"Yes, she can live in the dorm if she wants, and she will have support until she is 24 years-old if she follows the system. The state of California offers so many resources, as do federal grants, I want to make sure she gets the best support system around her."

"That sounds incredible. I would like to help her in any way I can with the school. If she decides to stay with USC, I can help. Maybe keep an eye on her. I feel a little more protective over her now."

"You're sweet. After watching the two of you together I think she would appreciate the comfort of knowing you were there. I know I would. She still has a long road ahead in counseling and healing from this. I hope she sticks with the counseling."

Maka laid her head on Alan's shoulder as he dried dishes.

"How long can you stay?"

"How long do you want me to stay?" she said jokingly.

Alan was drying the last dish. "Forever."

He looked Maka in the eyes. She blushed and started to fidget. Things got a little awkward for her, this was new for her. She had never been with a sensitive, caring, gentle man before.

"You don't mean that."

"I didn't mean to make you uncomfortable. I do mean it. Don't go. Stay here with me."

She walked out to the backyard, and he followed.

"This is complicated."

"It doesn't have to be."

"Relationships are always complicated. Someone always has to give up a piece of them, sacrifice for the other."

"Not true, in a relationship you complement each other, support one another, live your purpose together. Sure, there might be compromises or concessions once in a while. But it always balances out."

"Alan, we met under some very emotional circumstances."

"Stop, don't do this, the connection we felt, that we have, that's real. Don't minimalize that. It doesn't happen every day. Maka, I'm falling in love with you, I want to spend time with you, date you."

Maka didn't know what to say, she knew she was falling in love with him too. She also knew she needed to go back; she had a purpose to help her people.

"We've spent practically every day together for weeks. We've made love twice."

"Sex complicates everything," she added.

"Why does everything have to be so complicated for you? It seems simple to me, we love each other, and we want to be together. So, we figure out how to do that."

"Alan, I don't fit in your world, you're Hollywood. I'm from, well practically a third-world country in a way."

"So?"

Alan tried to be playful with her, he held her hand and walked with her around the backyard, they stopped and sat on a lounge chair by the pool. He sat first and pulled her down on his lap.

"It can be so easy."

"I have to think about Aiyana."

"Let me help."

Alan had a solution for every excuse Maka threw at him. She couldn't think of any other ways to debate, she was tired, and he was making a good argument. Alan was patient with her, he knew she was his soul match. It was easy for him, he surrendered to the flow they had and wanted to explore it deeper with her. They both knew they were from two different worlds in the material, but in the spirit, it felt easy, like home. They were torn between the passion and excitement of that honeymoon feeling and the true reality of what it might be or not be. They sat leaning, their foreheads pressed against one another, embraced in silence, both letting go of the chaos in their minds. Allowing the energy to flow between them. Their breath synced, becoming one. A magnet between their spirits, creating a warmth, a heat so powerful it was almost impossible to pull apart. They knew this could only be orchestrated by a higher power, a true soul connection.

Wikčémna Núŋpa Tópa

24

The sky was an endless blue, not a cloud to be found. Alan drove to the gate of the studio, having to stop at the guard's booth.

"Hello sir, how are you today?"

"Well, how are you, Joseph?

"I'm good thank you."

"Here for my meeting."

"Yes sir, I see you have an 11 o'clock."

"Yes."

"Thank you. Have a great day!"

Alan drove through the studio lot and found the parking spot with his name on it.

He walked to his office passing his secretary.

"Good morning, Sarah."

"Good morning, sir, good to have you back. Coffee?"

"No thank you."

He noticed a pile of mail on his large desk, behind it bookshelves lined with pictures and awards.

There was a large round table and chairs by the window and a full bathroom with a shower. He was distracted, thinking about Maka, he shuffled through the mail. There was a knock at the door. It was Jerry, he let himself in.

"There you are!"

He walked over and grabbed Alan's hand and pulled him in for a guy hug.

"Good to have you back. I want to hear all about it."

"You wouldn't believe me."

Jerry sat down and put his feet up on Alan's desk.

"What exactly is this meeting they called?"

Jerry put his hands behind his head.

"You know how they are, read through, make changes. Seems like the industry is changing daily these days. The streaming apps have changed everything."

"It's not like it used to be. My dad's era was lucky, those were the days. What I wouldn't give to have been a part of Hollywood then."

"Right. There was something more classic, an elegance. Not like that now."

"Not with those reality shows, don't get me started Jer."

"I know, I know. Damn, look at the time. I want to hear about your trip. You can tell me all about it after our meeting. We should start heading over."

"Right." Alan grabbed his things. "Jer, I want to write something more impactful, with meaning and purpose. Something that can make a difference. I understand now what Paythan was trying to accomplish, he is a hero."

Jerry held the door open for Alan.

"That might need to be an independent film buddy."

As Alan and Jerry were approaching the meeting room, he showed him a picture of Maka.

"She's beautiful."

"I know. I think I've fallen in love, Jer."

"Easy. You hardly know this woman."

"I know her better than you think."

Jerry shook his head, remembering how easily Alan fell in love with a sweet, pretty woman. He had seen his heart broken one too many times.

He opened the door to the meeting room. There were three men in suits sitting at the table with copies of the screenplay, glasses filled with water, and coffee mugs placed in front of them.

"Gentlemen, have a seat. We would like to do a read-through and make some changes.

Alan's stomach sank. He didn't realize it was that long of a meeting. He sat back in his chair with a pit in his stomach. He felt guilty leaving Maka and not helping her. She was working on contacting the agencies on Aiyana's behalf, making some headway in getting Aiyana set up with DCS.

Alan couldn't shake the feeling that he had let Maka and Aiyana down. He stepped away from his meeting and messaged Maka he would be later than he thought.

Night came, and Alan came home. The house was dark, only the light over the stove lit the kitchen. He was exhausted, dropped his bag in his office, slipped off his shoes, and walked to his bedroom. The door was closed, but a dim light illuminated the door. He slowly opened it and saw Maka cute as could be with her computer open next to her, she was sound asleep. He quietly slipped into the room and headed to the bathroom to shower.

The alarm clock read 3:33 am, Maka and Alan were in bed laying in each other's arms. Suddenly, Maka woke from her deep sleep, her eyes wide open, she turned and saw the time on the clock. She didn't want to alarm Alan, she slowly crawled out of bed. Throwing on a hoodie and some sweatpants, she made her way to the kitchen with her bag in hand, only turning on a small table lamp, she kept the room dim. She began to empty the evidence folders onto the table and sort through them.

She was talking to herself. *I know I'm missing something. What was Paythan trying to tell us? There is something more here, I just know it.*

She was looking at the obituaries, his term papers, and the photos. She still had one of the sticks she found at the grave site. She was hitting a dead end, she got up to make some tea. When she turned around, Aiyana startled her, she was standing in the shadows of the doorway.

"You startled me," Maka whispered.

"I'm sorry. Is that Paythan's?" Aiyana moved her way to the table, standing and looking over the organized clutter of evidence spread across. Maka finished filling the teapot with water and placed it on the stove.

"Yes," she realized the autopsy photos of Paythan were exposed. Before Aiyana saw them, she made her way over and nonchalantly covered them with some other paperwork. Aiyana was staring at the photos of the gravesite and looked over at the single stick on the table. She picked it up.

"Paythan used to make these."

"What did he use them for?"

"He was really into history and the stories of our people. Historically, he never told me exactly what they meant. He used it as markers when he and his friends would do vision quests. They did one when he got out of rehab this last time."

Maka poured the hot water into a mug with tea bags, she handed one to Aiyana, careful not to interrupt her.

"Do you know why Paythan was fixated on Crazy Horse?"

"He had an infatuation with Wounded Knee, I think he was determined to help the fight in getting back our land, like using his writing to make a documentary or something. The last time we talked about it was before the protest he said he had something big that he found on that last trip. He was going to write about it and expose it I guess."

Maka sat back down and shuffled through the pictures and papers. "The cemetery. That wasn't far from the hotel."

"Oh, no it wasn't far at all."

"Why would he go there?"

She showed Aiyana the obituaries, "Do you see anything here that looks familiar?"

"No, not really."

As they sat at the table, Maka looked over and noticed Aiyana seemed to be someplace else.

"Are you OK?"

She had to ask a couple of times before she got a response from Aiyana. She was nervous to open up to Maka but wondered if it might help.

"Maka?"

Maka, still studying the documents in front of her, responded with a soft "Yes?"

"I didn't tell you everything the other day."

"What do you mean, sweetie?"

Maka was a little distracted by what she was reading.

"Well, I didn't tell you everything about what happened."

"That's OK, do you want to share with me now?"

Maka lowered her reading glasses and looked up with soft, compassionate eyes.

"I think I better."

Maka felt a knot in her stomach. She looked at Aiyana, setting her paperwork aside, and the knot in her stomach started to grow. Aiyana was nervous, she started to fidget in her chair, her posture became very childlike, her arms went behind her back and she started to play with her fingers. Then she would shift and twist the ends of her long black hair around her finger.

"We didn't go right to Mexico."

She paused, struggling to make eye contact. Maka was very conscious to be still, to create a safe place for her.

"Well, they kept us at that hotel for days and then took us to other cities before we ended up in Tijuana. We tried to escape, made it across the river, and hid in the old drainpipe for a night. It was so cold, and we just wanted to go home. Dakota thought we could walk the road and maybe someone would give us a ride home. We walked for a couple of hours, not knowing where we were, and ended up going in the wrong direction. A tribal officer pulled up to us in one of those pickup trucks. We were so excited to see him. He seemed understanding and like he wanted to help us. He made us both sit in the back; I was relieved to be going home. But he didn't take us home, he took us right back to the hotel. One of the men from inside came out and they handcuffed us. He shoved Dakota and me on the ground, and started kicking us, he kicked her so hard in the face she spit out teeth."

She stopped for a moment, collecting herself, Maka got her some water and moved to the chair next to her.

"I'm sorry," Maka tried to console her. Quickly, she realized she should be still and silent.

Aiyana felt sick, she knew she needed to tell her what happened, it was harder than she thought it was going to be. The more she tried to remember, the more she was reliving the pain. She was trying to decide if she could continue.

"I, I may not tell it in the right order. Maybe I should stop."

"It's OK. If you want to continue, don't worry about it. Just get it out if you want to."

Aiyana took a small sip of water. She nodded.

"OK." She picked up a pen and was scribbling on a piece of paper. Maka just sat with her. A few minutes passed and she started to share more of her story. Maka knew how important it was to support her and help her find her voice.

"They blindfolded us, took us back inside. I could tell it was the same room I was in before we ran away. Had the same disgusting smell, and I will never forget it. They didn't feed us. Then the next day they forced us into a car, blindfolded us, and took us someplace. They wouldn't let us talk but I knew there were other girls in the car with me. There were men there, some spoke our native language, and some didn't. They put me in a room and took off the handcuffs and the blindfold came off. A man came into the room and tried to push me onto the bed, I fought as hard as I could, another one came in and then the officer came in again. He was angry, he handcuffed me, blindfolded me, and made me lay on the bed… I don't know if I can do this."

Aiyana was tearing up, unable to look Maka in the eyes.

"It's OK, you can tell me whatever you want, whenever you want."

They sat in silence, Aiyana scribbled more on her paper. Maka sat patiently and watched her, she gave her a little time to gather herself. She was sympathetic and knew how hard this was for her.

Aiyana started to talk softly again.

"This went on for a couple of days. They put us back in the vehicle again, took us to an apartment someplace, and as our reward, they took us to a football game. I have never been to one before, I liked football and used to watch it with my Auntie and the boys. It was our fun time together."

Aiyana scribbled again. Maka got up, "Tea?"

"Yes."

Maka made them some tea and they took a little break. Then she asked, "What happened at the football game?"

"After the game, they took us to a party with the players. I thought it was so cool, the athletes, you see on TV. They always seem so nice to kids on the field. But at the party, they were expecting us to do things for them. There was even a boy there doing things. I asked for help, but no one would help. It wasn't the only time they took us to games and parties after. The more I fought the more they beat me and wouldn't feed me."

She got up and walked away from the table, Maka wasn't sure where she went. She sat for a moment wondering if she was coming back. Shortly after Aiyana walked up to Maka and handed her a pocket-size notebook, the kind with the wire rings binding it together. Maka took it and looked at her empathetically.

"You can read this, but you probably won't understand it. I took notes of the places they would take us. I wrote it so if they found it, they wouldn't understand what it is, it's my story. I wrote down landmarks and started to learn their patterns. If something happened, I hoped if someone did find it, they could find where I was."

"This is incredible, Aiyana. I'm so proud of you. How many other girls were in the apartment with you?"

"About fifteen. There was a lot of drinking and drugs. I chose not to. I prayed a lot to the spirit guides. They took us to strip clubs and stuff."

"Was Dakota in the apartment with you?"

"At first. She started taking drugs and drinking. There were a lot of fights between the girls who had been there a while and the newbies."

Maka poured more tea for them.

"When was the last time you saw her?"

"The last time I tried running away again. I was in a city. I didn't know anything. I was lost. I was hiding in a parking garage; I didn't know what to do. I had no phone or money."

She paused again. Maka was so impressed with Aiyana's strength and shared that to break the silence.

"I don't know what to say. You have been so resilient."

Maka flipped through her notebook and then set it down.

"Where did you go after the parking garage?"

"I was hungry, started walking through the city, so many people. Someone gave me some money for food. I started walking, trying to find help and they found me, beat me and that's when the next thing I remember I woke in Tijuana. They put me in a room with three other girls, they told me to stop running. One girl they cut her back of the ankle, think called some kind of tendons so she couldn't run anymore."

"Achilles tendons" Maka chimed in.

"Yes, that's it."

Maka reached across and comforted Aiyana with a small hug.

"I'm so proud of you."

They hugged but then Aiyana quickly pulled away.

"There is more in the notebook. Do you think it could help find Dakota?"

"It might."

"I did hear someone talking about wanting to slow things down on the Reservation and use another reservation. Chief Hurd was mad. I heard him threaten the men who said they were not going to be doing business with him."

"Did they say why?"

"What I heard was too much attention on the Reservation, and they felt it was too risky."

"This was while you were in Tijuana?"

"Yeah."

The time was going by quickly, and they both sat back in their chairs stretching.

"Oh god, the sun is coming up."

Aiyana got up to stretch, walked over to the counter, and took a cookie. She walked back to the table taking another glance over everything, one of the photos of Paythan's murder scene was partially exposed.

"Maka, what did that obituary say again?"

Maka pulled out the obituary and read it to her. "William Bunch, nee Fearing the Hawk, died from a rattlesnake bite Thursday. He was nineteen years old. He will be laid to rest at Whispering Cedar Cemetery Saturday at seven PM, Section 7D. He asks to please make note of his new address."

Aiyana stared at a photo on the table for a moment. "Paythan…"

"Oh, honey don't look at those." Maka quickly covered the photo.

"I'm OK." She pulled out the picture that was under it, it was a photo Maka had taken at Whispering Cedar.

"This war lance was our great grandfather's. Paythan left it there?"

"I found it near the grave."

"Weird. Ummm, should there be fresh graves dug here?"

Maka looked at the picture. She stared for a moment; Aiyana might be right. It was hard to be sure but there were two areas in the photo that looked recently disturbed. "What was going on here, grave robbers?"

Alan came into the room, "Good morning. You girls are up early. I smelled coffee."

"Good morning." Aiyana reciprocated.

"Good morning, I didn't mean to wake you." Maka got up and hugged him.

"You didn't. What's all this? I thought I heard grave robbers?"

Alan poured a cup of coffee, walked over, and looked at the table.

"I don't know why we didn't catch this when we were there, but there seemed to be a new grave site dug."

"Really, why?"

"That's what I'm trying to figure out. Supposedly there hasn't been an interment in twenty years."

"Paythan do it? He was curious, but I don't think he would disturb the resting place of his ancestors."

Maka looked at the picture more intently. "I need to make a phone call."

Alan and Aiyana were puzzled and continued to look through the pictures. Maka stepped away to call McKenzie.

"McKenzie, what are you doing?"

"Your paperwork."

"Well stop and take a ride to Whispering Cedar Cemetery. Don't tell anyone. Call me when you get there."

"I'll go after…" Maka cut her off.

"Go now. Please."

"Ok. I'll figure something out."

"Call me as soon as you get there and be careful. Oh, and bring a shovel." Maka hung up the phone and jumped in the shower. Alan and Aiyana stepped outside to drink their coffee.

"So, I never asked, are you still in high school?"

"No, I just graduated. Well, I missed my graduation but…"

"I'm sorry."

Aiyana stared off into the distance, Alan felt like he put his foot in his mouth. He was relieved when Maka come out and joined them.

"You showered."

"Yes, we have a big day ahead for all of us."

***

McKenzie arrived at the cemetery. She wasn't getting any cell service. She thought to herself, *Figures.* She got out and started walking around, trying to find service and maybe notice why Maka sent her there. She found a spot where she had service, she started to dial when she heard something in the brush behind her. She turned slowly as she heard the rattling. Reaching for her gun, she couldn't see anything under the grass and dried leaves, but she could hear it. *Always something,* she said to herself. "OK, where are you?" she stepped slowly backward about four or five steps. Tripping on something, she almost fell. She looked down noticing the ground was soft, there were chunks of grass laid on top of a grave site. She had forgotten about the snake for a second until she caught it slithering going in the opposite direction. She tried dialing Maka again.

"Maka. I'm here, service is horrible."

"Ok. Can you find the seventh row, four up? Then check the nearby graves there."

"Wait, tell me what I am looking for in case we lose connection."

"For a new grave. That cemetery hasn't been touched in over twenty years."

"Grave robbers looking for artifacts?"

"Just go take a look. I have a hunch."

"I knew I should have changed my shoes. The things I do for you Mahpiya."

"You love me, just do it."

"Text me if I lose you and keep calling back."

Maka texted her the plot number and row information she had.

"I got it."

McKenzie walked over to the area she pointed out, and sure enough, the ground was loose and there appeared to be a fresh plot. There didn't appear to be anyone around. McKenzie thought to herself, *This is why she said to bring a shovel.*

"You still there?"

"Yes, I think I found it. It's definatley fresh but there is grass laid back down on it."

"Did you bring a shovel?"

"Uh, yes but…"

"Well, start digging."

"Maka, there is more than one and I don't think a shovel is going to do it." McKenzie surveyed the area and saw several areas with new grass growing and one was just bare dirt, no new growth.

"I think we need the team."

"Ok, don't touch anything, and don't say anything to anyone."

"I can call in the team."

"You know if the evidence is moved it's not as authentic."

"We will video and take pictures."

"The quality won't be the same if it's moved. I will get the next flight out."

Maka immediately hung up and made flight arrangements. She wasn't sure how she was going to break the news to Alan. She found him in his bathroom shaving.

"Alan, I'm sorry. I got a call and have to get back to the Res. Someone from DCS is coming today to pick up Aiyana."

"You have to go now? I don't understand. She can stay until they get things arranged. If she wants."

"I must keep her in my custody, or she has to go to DCS. She's not eighteen yet."

"When will you be back?"

"I'm not sure. Once this investigation is over. I don't want to leave. I have to." Alan was crushed.

"I can take you to the airport at least."

"It may interfere with your meeting."

"This is more important than that, what time is your flight?"

"2:30 pm was the soonest I could find one."

"Ok, what time is DCS coming?"

"I'm not sure. They said between now and noon."

"Oh. Burbank airport, right?"

"Oh, yes."

"OK, good…LAX is horrible."

Aiyana came into the room.

"What's going on?"

"There has been a change of plans. DCS is this afternoon instead of tomorrow. I have to leave tonight for the Res."

"I don't want to go."

"You have to, I can't leave you here."

"Why can't I stay with Alan?"

"Because you are not eighteen yet."

"Please don't make me."

Aiyana ran to her room and slammed the door. Maka followed her and motioned to Alan to stay.

He walked away slowly, Maka watched him as she collected herself to go in and talk to Aiyana. She knocked and opened the door slowly.

"I'm sorry, but you knew you would have to go eventually. It will only be for a short time. Then you would have a choice, when you turn eighteen you can go wherever you want. Would you rather go back to the Reservation?"

"*No!* I want to stay here and go to USC this fall. I turn eighteen at the end of September."

"Ok, that's not that far away. We will make all the arrangements. I promise. When I come back, we will get it all worked out."

Aiyana got up and started to pace.

"Why can't you stay?"

"Sweetie, I have to go back, have to try and make sure this doesn't happen again. The fact we found you beat all odds. A typical case, Aiyana, is if you don't find someone in 48 to 72 hours, chances is you won't. Paythan's clues helped lead us to you. He lost his life, but you still have yours. The journey you choose now, your healing journey, and what you do moving forward will be in honor of him."

Aiyana sat next to Maka on the edge of her bed.

"I have already looked into it. I found a great counseling program for you, there are grants for school, housing, medical, and everything you will need. You will have to follow the system, but the majority of your expenses will be covered until you are 24 years old. We can discuss it later."

Feeling numb, lost, and alone, all Aiyana could do is pick up her bag and start to pack the few items she had. Her mind raced, and she thought to herself, just a few months ago she was planning her trip to start college this fall, a new life with her brother. Now her world had completely changed before she was even eighteen. She was still a child who was forced into a dark, evil adult world she never thought could happen to her. She was a good kid she thought to herself, she never did drugs or hung out with the gangs or the kids that got into trouble all the time. She stayed clean.

Maka had written a note to leave for Alan, she made sure it was visible on the kitchen counter.

When DCS arrived at Alan's, the case worker went over everything with Maka and Aiyana. It was difficult for Maka. She felt a tremendous responsibility to still protect Aiyana, and yet she knew this would be best for her at the moment. She went over every scenario in her mind of how she could make it work and bring Aiyana with her. At the same time, she knew in her spirit Aiyana needed professional help at this crucial time to heal and have a chance for a healthy future. Aiyana's eyes filled with tears as they started to walk out the door, she turned and looked at Maka.

"I will be back soon. I promise."

Maka reached for her and gave her a sisterly hug.

"Thank you," Aiyana said holding back the tears. She followed the case-worker to her car parked on the side of the house.

As they pulled away, she noticed she missed a text from Alan. He was apologizing he could not leave the meeting to take her to the airport. As Maka closed the door, a black Cadillac Escalade arrived at his house to pick her up.

There was a knock at the door. Maka opened it to find a man in a white button-down shirt, black tie, and black pants, black shoes freshly polished.

"Ms. Mahpiya, Mr. Fitzgerald sent me. I'm here to take you to the airport."

Wikčémna Núŋpa Záptaŋ

25

The plane had landed in Rapid City, and McKenzie picked up Maka. They drove for a moment in silence as Maka was reading through messages on her phone.

"What is the plan, Mahpiya?"

"After I reviewed the photos you sent earlier, we are going to need more than a shovel and just the two of us."

"What if it is just grave robbers? We don't want to call in a whole team."

"What if it's not?" Maka added.

"We should go check it out first," McKenzie was adamant about confirming their suspicions before calling it in.

Alan was being kept at the office; the producers wanted revisions, some of which were killing Alan to have to make. All he could think about was how the studio producers could make a mess out of a well-written screenplay. It was all about what they felt would sell and make the biggest return, taking away from the message and art. Ironically, they were not always right, and it flopped when they did this.

McKenzie pulled into the front of the cemetery. The sun had almost set, and it was getting dark quickly. They each grabbed a shovel from the back of the vehicle, a black equipment bag, and a couple of flashlights.

Picking the most recently disturbed spot that she found, they began to dig. Almost two feet down their shovels hit something. Using the flashlight, they could see it was a black garbage bag. Gently, they started to remove the dirt. There was already a rank, putrid smell coming from the bag. Both were speechless, all they could hear was the sound of chirping frogs surrounding the area.

Maka reached over and took out a utility knife from their equipment bag. She slowly cut into the bag, trying to hold her breath. McKenzie pulled her shirt over her nose and mouth; it didn't change the sweet sickly smell. Opening the bag revealed a young boy, the body expanding from the gases building up inside. He was Native, Maka guessed twelve or thirteen.

"What the hell!" she said.

She was just as shocked as Maka.

"This is not what I thought we were going to find."

Maka slowly lifted herself from the hole, trying not to disturb the area for evidence.

"Let's call it in."

"Well, guess they didn't think anyone would look in an old historical cemetery."

"Except for maybe a young man on a historical search for truth for his people. Paythan was in way over his head."

***

It was after eight o'clock in California, Alan was just getting home. He walked into his dark, empty house, and tossed his car keys into the little bowl he had gotten from Africa on the credenza by the front door. He dropped his bag, looked around the lonely room, and decided to go and change. Checking his phone again, still no messages from Maka, he put on some sweatpants and a hoodie. He walked into the living room and flopped on the couch, dropped his phone next to him, and stared at the dark fireplace. *God, I miss her,* he thought to himself.

***

The U.S. Marshals took the lead in the investigation at Whisper Cedars with the help and guidance of tribal historians and tribal officers in navigating through the historical site. Maka wanted to ensure they showed the utmost respect for the area and the pre-existing grave sites there.

They limited their search for the night to only the sites that appeared more recently disturbed. The team brought in the balloon lighting and spotlights. They had specially trained people digging with shovels and a bobcat. The Deputy Chief pulled Maka and McKenzie aside.

"Nice work. We will need to wait for daylight to be able to assess this you know."

"Yes, sir."

As they were talking, someone yelled from off in the distance, "Deputy you need to come to take a look at this."

The three of them walked over quickly, stopping on the edge and looking into the hole, there were several bodies piled on top of one another, some skeletons and some still decaying. All appeared to be young children of all ages.

"What the hell. Hart, over here." Deputy Chief waved for the forensic photographer and agent to come over.

***

Alan had no idea what Maka was going through and sulked, missing her, he had his laptop now and was typing away, he appeared to be working on his screenplay. His phone rang, he quickly picked it up, it was Jerry.

"Hey, Jer."

"Hi, are you alone?"

"Yes, they're gone."

"So, the producers love the re-write its green lit. We just made it, nice job."

"Thanks."

Alan got up and walked to the kitchen, he lifted the tea kettle, which had water in it, so he started the stove.

"You'll be in the office tomorrow morning, right?"

"Yes, Jer."

"Good. We can talk about that other project you mentioned. Let's grab happy hour tomorrow. Celebrate!"

"Maybe." Alan pulled a coffee mug from the cupboard, he walked past Maka's note and didn't notice it.

"Have a good night. See you tomorrow."

They hung up the phone, Jer, so self-absorbed, he hardly noticed how quiet Alan was and unresponsive.

Morning couldn't come quick enough for Alan, he couldn't sleep. Sitting in his office writing, he looked at the time, 4:20 a.m. He counted to himself, 6:00 a.m. in South Dakota. He pushed away from the computer, stopped at the bathroom, making his way to the kitchen. Looking in the cupboards, "Don't tell me I'm out of coffee." There was nothing there. He looked at the coffee pot, there he saw the note Maka left leaning up against the bag of coffee beans. Clever girl, he thought. For the moment he forgot about making coffee and read her note.

Dear Alan, I'm sorry I had to leave so quickly. I hope your meeting was a great success. We are very much alike in that our careers are a part of who we are, and more our purpose than a job. I have so much I would like to say to you, but I'm not a writer like you and the words escape me, as it is more of what I feel and know in my spirit than what I can put into words. When I look into your eyes, I see your soul and it feels like home to me. You feel like home to me. A place that is not that familiar, but it feels safe, it feels right. See you soon. Iyuha ma chante. Iyotanja M~ (With all my heart, Love).

Alan smiled and read it a few times. He took it into his office and pinned it on the corkboard right behind his computer screen.

***

The sun was up, equipment and people were everywhere, and police tape blocked off certain areas where they had finished digging. The daylight revealed what once was a peaceful, desolate historic cemetery; now appeared to be a post-war zone. The investigators had found numerous remains belonging to mostly young Native women. Everyone working the scene was in disbelief. They talked amongst themselves, all asking the same kind of questions. How long has this been going on? Who has been behind it all?

Maka knew this investigation was far from over. It was going to take weeks for them to process a scene of this magnitude. This was just a small dent in something much bigger. She couldn't stop thinking about some of the girls that she had come across during this investigation. She wanted to go back and help the ones that were asking for help. She didn't know how she was going to get that approved, but she was determined to try.

Deputy Chief called her over. "You have new orders that just came in." "Yes sir."

"You need to go and tie up loose ends with your witnesses and close the files from CBX. We will be continuing to process this scene. McKenzie will take things over here while you handle the other. When you get back, there will be a debriefing and the next step in this investigation. You have three days to get it done and be back here."

"Sir, there is still the missing girl, Dakota, and a few other girls that asked for help. Can I proceed and go back to Tijuana?"

"No. Submit your report and you will have to submit all the proper documentation for approval."

"Sir, when can I interview some of the suspects we took into custody?"

"When the F.B.I. is through and says you can, unfortunately. Ok, that's all. You need to get back to the office."

Deputy Chief walked away talking to some of the other agents. Maka approached McKenzie.

"What was that all about?"

"You need to take me back to the office; I'll fill you in on the way.

We have a new adventure, brush up on your Spanish. We are going to Tenancingo."

McKenzie looked at Maka, stunned.

"Just get in the car McKenzie," Maka smirked.

As they drove, Maka drifted off lost in thought, reflecting on how frustrating working in a male-dominated industry was and how much harder she and the other women had to work. She remembered a story her grandmother told her when it was the women who made the decisions. They had the say in if a man would lead their tribe.

"Earth to Maka, boy, where are you?" McKenzie noticed how distant she seemed.

"Oh, sorry. I was just lost in thought."

"Clearly. Anything you can share?"

"I honestly don't know why I was thinking it. Just how challenging working in a male-dominated industry is. How hard they make it for women to even work together. It's like they keep a wedge between women making it harder for them to work together, support each other."

"We work well together."

"We do, but how many other women can you say that about?"

"True, a lot of competition. It doesn't have to be that way."

"Right. My grandmother told me a story back in the day how the women were the leaders, and they could take a man out of power."

"Wow, that would be incredible. Women are better at leading, serving their communities; they're more generous."

"I agree, I think if women would come together more our world would be free from some of the poverty and hopelessness that is here. It would be different, there would be less trafficking. If only people realized how much power they truly have." Maka seemed to grow in her seat, shifting as her passion for her beliefs started to radiate through her pours. McKenzie noticed a glow, as her soul took over.

"Think about it, if they stopped buying the crap food, then the prices would come down on healthier food and they wouldn't make as much junk food. If women came together to support each other on a deeper level, maybe women wouldn't end up in those narcissistic, abusive relationships or feel they can't support themselves unless they sell themselves for sex." Maka added.

Maka's energy was contagious and McKenzie felt an overwhelming feeling to share. "It would definitely teach the younger generation more self-worth, and self-respect. Heck, I'm forty-two years old and just now learning boundaries. No one taught me growing up."

"Me too."

"I agree with you. If more women could come together, set aside the competition and that wedge that has been created over generations, we would all be much further." McKenzie said with conviction.

Maka started to feel vulnerable. "Sorry, I get on my soapbox...could talk about this all day."

"Don't be sorry, I appreciate being able to talk about this with someone who understands it too."

"It is nice to have a safe place to speak your heart."

There was a brief silence, as they reflected for a moment. McKenzie wanted to change the subject.

"Did you say you had a nice chat with Aiyana?"

"Yes." Maka answered quickly. "She shared some things about her and

Paythan. He seemed to have a good head on his shoulders. So does she. They had plans, they wanted an education, and they were at the protest a while back fighting for the land and the missing women. They were bringing hope back to the Res. Here are two kids, who against all odds are still fighting for the greater good, and then they have to go through this."

"As challenging as it seems, we both know sometimes we go through these situations, and it brings us out stronger with our story we can help people rise up and bring hope. You don't know, Aiyana could turn this around and use it to help fuel her efforts in what she was already fighting for."

Maka could relate. "I agree, if I didn't go through what I did, I wouldn't have learned the compassion and all that I did to be able to serve as I do. It was a driving force and helped me to relate and be relatable."

"It's all about perception. And healing, rising out of victim to survivor to that safe place in our soul and our mind. I feel like Aiyana is that type of girl, like her brother."

McKenzie chimed in. "It sounds like she won't stay a victim, she will heal, and it will empower her more, strengthen her voice."

"I hope so, I have seen so many girls who stay a victim and use that victim mentality for the rest of their lives. Whether be for attention, manipulation, and even to make money from it. Then you have the women who do the work, heal, and step into their power. A true voice to help bring others to a safe place. There is a difference."

McKenzie agreed. "I can see your point."

She was so engrossed in the conversation they passed their office.

"What is happening in our world?"

"I don't know. But I do know you passed the office like half a mile ago."

They both started laughing, the kind of laugh that was more stress relief. The conversation was getting heavy and Maka felt she could use a little time to clear her mind.

***

Alan was working back on the studio lot; he was having difficulty concentrating. He found himself daydreaming out the window. The last few weeks seemed so dreamlike. This immoral, sick, twisted, evil that existed was a part of a dark world he never believed was real. How could such ungodly, wicked, cruel people even exist? Sure, he heard stories of these things, about corruption, trafficking, and abuse. He read books and saw movies. But he had never experienced it in real life. He would never be the same. It was a bittersweet journey, he didn't regret any of it, but he also was having difficulty digesting the past few weeks. He didn't know how to process any of it, didn't know what to do with the emotions he felt, the memories and dreams he was having from what he had witnessed. He felt he was going through a withdrawal of sorts. Maybe from all the stress, cortisol, and adrenaline. He was starting to feel very lethargic, distracted, and a little lost. He realized, *I am not built for this stuff.* He wondered how Maka and others in that profession handled it if they felt like this after a big case or incident.

***

McKenzie pulled into the back of the Sheriff's Department. As she and Maka walked around the corner of the building they were surrounded by a few reporters.

"You're the Marshall that found the girls. Right?"

Maka and McKenzie tried to walk past them without answering their questions. Each one yelled out question after question, so fast they could hardly understand them. Supervising Deputy Chief Marshal came outside, stopping them.

"Ladies, let's take a moment and answer some questions." He placed his hand on Maka's shoulder, turning her toward the camera. He intercepted a few questions but left her answering one.

"What is it like finding the girls?"

Maka looked at McKenzie and then the reporters, she took a deep breath.

"Well, it's hard to put into words, what we feel when we rescue a child. I can tell you that this operation has impacted every single one of us out here. We are working to protect them and get them the help they need. That's all I can say right now."

She turned abruptly before she started to get emotional, pushing past her supervisor, leaving him to finish answering their questions. That was what he loved most, being in front of the camera, the media, and the attention. He would do whatever he could to have his camera time.

Wikčémna Núŋpa Šákpe

26

A few days passed, and Alan was looking forward to Maka's return. He was waiting at the airport to pick her up. He pulled up to the baggage area and saw her off in the distance, he drove up as quickly as he could. He got out quickly to help her with her luggage.

"Hi. How was your flight?"

"Hi. It was OK."

There was a bit of awkwardness between them, the time apart made it both exciting for them to reunite and a little awkward at the same time. Alan leaned in to kiss her, she was shy and clumsy, and they missed each other's lips. He ended up kissing her eyes, she hugged him, and they laughed.

"We better go. Holding up traffic."

Alan wrote their reuniting in his head much better than how it went. He wished they could have a 'take two.'

"Do you mind dropping me at the office in Westwood? Like I mentioned, they will be waiting for me."

"You must be hungry. Time for lunch?"

"Unfortunately, I do not. Dinner possibly? They sent someone to pick up my vehicle, right?"

"Yes, the same day you left."

"They only gave me three days here and then I have to get back."

Alan reached and took hold of her hand; he kissed the back of it.

"I missed you."

"I missed you too." She rested her cheek on the back of his hand.

He dropped her at the federal building in Westwood and went back to his office at the studio. Maka spent hours filling out reports, she didn't leave the office until nine o'clock. She messaged Alan to let him know she was on her way.

Maka knocked on the front door at Alan's. He opened it, "You don't have to knock."

She smiled. He kissed her on the cheek, "Let me help you with your bag."

"If it's OK, I'd like to take a quick shower." She could smell some amazing food cooking in the kitchen. There was a glow of a string of lights coming through the kitchen window.

"Yes, of course. I'll finish dinner. Come join me when you're ready."

Maka disappeared into the bathroom. A little over twenty minutes later she came out. Alan had seemed to disappear, and the stove was off. She heard some dishes clanking outside and walked to the back door, Alan opened it slowly.

"Hi. You look beautiful."

The patio was lit by a string of lights outlining the frame of the patio. He had the table set, candles lit, a beautiful bouquet of at least three dozen roses in the center. It was almost a full moon. He had a glass soda bottle of Sprite and a wine glass in front of her plate and his. The whole thing was beautiful and romantic.

"Looks beautiful, thank you."

He walked her to her chair and pulled it out for her and handed her the napkin. He cooked an amazing meal, his special poached salmon with dill sauce, wild rice, and asparagus, and for dessert, he had a decadent flourless chocolate cake.

They stayed up for hours talking and re-acquainting. It was the first time since they had met that they could have an uninterrupted, intimate conversation.

Maka saw the time, it was 2:30 am.

"I don't want this night to end. Thank you, Alan. This has been amazing, you did too much."

"I wanted to do more, had I had a little more time."

"We should try and get some sleep. I have to be in the office by eight in the morning."

"Yes, of course."

They both cleared off the table enough that the rest could wait until morning.

"DCS said we can pick up Aiyana around 3:30, take her to dinner. I need to talk to you both about the next steps. But that's then."

"Don't forget tomorrow evening is the red-carpet event I mentioned."

"You did. I almost forgot." She didn't forget; she was hoping he would. "Do we need to go?"

"Yes." He was disappointed she wasn't more excited. "Do you not want to go now?"

"It's fine. I just don't have anything to wear."

"I thought you might say that. I took the liberty of having my PA pick you up a few options. I hope you don't mind. They are hanging in the guest room."

She was stunned and didn't know what to say. She wasn't sure how she should feel, flattered that he took the time and was thoughtful, or should she be offended that he sent another woman shopping for her clothes? She decided to try and stay positive and look at it as if he was being thoughtful and sweet, knowing she was out of her element, never having attended an event like this before.

"Please go and see if you like any of them. If you don't, we can find you something tomorrow."

She went to the guest room, three garment bags were hanging. She approached them slowly as if it was a wild mustang she wanted to tame. Unzipping the bags, she lined up each dress, there were two black and one red, very elegant, yet simple dresses. Below were two pairs of shoes to choose from, very sexy heels. She thought to herself that his assistant was spot on, and they hadn't even met. She started to feel something deep down, like the little girl inside of her wanted to play dress up. She tried each dress on, and two of them fit her like a glove, she looked at herself in the mirror finding the one she felt most comfortable in. She tried on the shoes, surprised again, another perfect fit. She stood again looking in the mirror, she couldn't believe that the woman in the mirror was her. It was like a fairytale, she never imagined she would ever be wearing such a beautiful dress and going to a big Hollywood party. *If these moments were a movie, she thought to herself, I just went from a thriller, crime drama to a romantic Disney theme.* There was a tap on the door. *And there is my prince,* she laughed to herself.

"Everything okay?"

"Yes, I will be out in a minute."

Quickly, she stepped back into her clothes and hung the dresses back up in their garment bags, replacing the shoes in their boxes. It appeared she hadn't even touched them. She opened the door and started to walk towards the kitchen, Alan met her partway.

"So do you like any of them?"

"Yes, I think there is one that will be fine. Do I need to do anything special with my hair or…?"

"If you would like, we have a tentative appointment with the stylist tomorrow before the event. He will do your hair and makeup. You don't need to; you are absolutely beautiful and perfect. I just wanted to make it easy for you, knowing how busy you are, and how hard you have been working. Completely up to you."

"Oh, can I think about it?"

"Of course." Alan put his arm around Maka and guided her to the bedroom.

It seemed they had just closed their eyes and it was already morning. Maka and Alan jumped out of bed, they overslept. It was 7:15 am, "We have to go."

They got dressed quickly. Maka kissed Alan, "See you later, I will text you."

They ran out the door together. Alan had to get to the studio, Maka the field office.

As the day progressed, Maka was stressing herself out thinking about the event that evening. She was nervous, going over and over in her mind that she didn't want to let Alan down. At the very last moment, she decided to go to the appointment and have her hair done.

She arrived at the salon in Beverly Hills, it was valet parking. She stepped inside, looked around and thought to herself, *What did I do?* A young woman who looked like she was straight out of the movie *Pretty Woman* approached just bursting with energy.

"You must be Ms. Mahpiya. I'm Jen, Alan told us all about you, please follow me."

She led Maka to a private room. "There is a dressing room right here, you can put on a cape in there. Can I get you something to drink, cappuccino, water, champagne?"

Maka didn't know what to say, all she could think was, *Where the hell am I?*

"Water, thank you."

"Flat, sparkling, mineral?"

Maka felt like she wanted to crawl out of her skin. "Surprise me." She walked into the dressing room, removed her suit jacket, and put on the cape over her shirt and gun holster. As she came out of the room she walked into a very energetic and flamboyant man.

"Maka! You are beautiful! Alan didn't tell us how beautiful you were. We are going to have so much fun!"

He walked towards her and began running his fingers through her hair.

"You have such beautiful hair, and your skin is like satin. I know just what we are going to do for this evening. You will love it!"

He guided her to his chair and began to sculpt his masterpiece. Maka felt a pit in her stomach, she knew it was too late to leave, and she had to go through with it.

Back at Alan's house, she arrived before he got home. She went straight to the guest room to get dressed. As she walked past a mirror, she had to do a double take, she thought to herself. *Who is this? I don't even recognize myself.*

Alan rushed into the house, the door slamming behind him.

"I'm sorry I'm late" he yelled through the house. "I will just be a minute, going to hop in the shower." Maka stayed in the bedroom staring at herself in the mirror, responding, "OK. I will be ready when you are."

Moments later, Alan was standing at the front door waiting for Maka.

"Ready when you are." He had a single rose in hand thinking to himself, I can't ever remember feeling this nervous, not even at my first wedding. He could feel his palms sweating and just as he was about to go get a drink of water Maka appeared. The low-lit room extenuated the lines of her figure, the black dress outlined every curve. She stood shyly, not sure what to do. Alan walked towards her. His mouth felt like it was full of cotton balls. Handing her the rose, he kissed her gently on the back of her hand and looked her in the eyes. "You are radiant."

She noticed his flawless tux; he looked so Hollywood.

"Thank you. You look handsome."

"Excuse me I need to get some water. Would you like some?"

"Yes, please."

Alan returned with two bottles of water, extending his arm to her. "Shall we? Maka took his arm as he escorted her to the car. She never had a man show her this level of chivalry before, she found herself getting lost in the romance. This was out of her comfort zone but at the same time, she felt safe, a sense of comfort by his side.

They arrived at the event located on the studio lot. The valet opened Alan's door, and he quickly went around to Maka's door and helped her out. Photographers swarmed the red carpet, and bright lights lit the way into the building. Maka took Alan's arm, squeezing it so tight, it felt like she was going to cut off his circulation. He thought to himself, *She is freakishly strong. I feel bad she is so nervous.* The photographers made them stop several times on their way to the event. Maka looked at Alan, he whispered in her ear "Just a couple of pictures, you look amazing." Maka thought to herself, *I would rather be in cowboy boots right now chasing bad guys.* This was a world she had never been exposed to and never in her dreams thought she would.

The area was flooded with celebrities dressed in a variety of designer dresses and suits. Spotlights lined the red carpet reflecting their jewelry. The flashes from all the cameras were blinding and Maka could hardly hear a word Alan was saying. Inside was more crowded than the outside, people scattered around greeting each other, while others were busy taking selfies. Maka thought to herself, *I will just observe and watch the show.* She couldn't believe her eyes, she read about these parties and saw them on Entertainment Tonight, but this was nothing like what they showed on television.

She wanted to enjoy the evening and tried to be supportive, though she felt completely out of her element. She sat back and observed Alan as he worked the room, it was like a dance for him, effortlessly flowing from one conversation to the next. This was a different side of him that she hadn't seen, he hadn't stopped smiling once, and he looked so happy. There was something different about him here, he was in his element.

Alan caught Maka watching him from across the room, she was sitting at a table in light conversation with a couple who were seated there. He smiled, and she smiled back, he excused himself from the conversation and made his way to Maka, extending his hand to help her up, escorting her to the dance floor.

"Oh no, no I can't dance."

"Just follow my lead."

"No, really I don't know how to dance like this."

"Trust me. Just like this…"

She had no choice but to surrender, he already began dancing; his rhythm guided her feet. The more she let go, the more in sync they were, and she glided along in sync with him. Before she knew it, he had her doing the tango.

The party was coming to an end. They waited in line at the valet.

"Hungry?" Alan asked.

"I could snack."

"I noticed you hardly touched your dinner."

"Guess I was a little nervous."

"Well, it wouldn't be a true Hollywood night if we didn't stop at In and Out Burger."

"I have never tried one."

The car had arrived, and the valet held the door open for Maka.

"Well, you are in for a treat."

Arriving back at Alan's he opened the door for her and handed her back her stiletto shoes. She had taken them off in the car.

"Thank you, my feet are killing me. I don't know how women wear these regularly."

"I'm just glad I don't have to," he laughed.

Maka put her shoes down and walked up to him, wrapping her arms around his waist.

"Thank you. For tonight. For everything."

"You're welcome. You were quiet on the way home. Everything ok?"

"I didn't feel like I fit in your world until I realized you are the world where I fit. I found safety in that and like our dance, I learned to surrender to the flow of it, to expand and grow with it, much like the current in a river. The less I tried to fight it the easier and more peaceful it became. Thank you."

"Not sure if you knew this, I felt the same way in your world. You said it perfectly, once I surrendered and was open to a new perspective, once I realized it was you, I could rest in that, trust in you and the journey."

They embraced for a moment longer.

Wikčémna Núŋpa Šakówiŋ

27

The day was slipping by, 3:30 came, and Maka and Alan arrived at the shelter. They walked up to the front desk; Alan had never experienced a place like this, it was in a rough neighborhood. It was clean, with people coming and going, cameras everywhere, and gated.

Aiyana was being escorted to the front by her case worker, she looked rested. She was wearing new clothes and seemed in good spirits from afar.

"Hello. How are you?" Maka walked towards her, and they hugged. Alan excited to see her walked up behind Maka and hugged Aiyana.

"Hungry?"

"Starving," Aiyana replied.

Maka stepped aside to speak to the case worker. Alan distracted Aiyana and walked with her.

"What are you hungry for?"

"Italian."

"Ok, Italian it is. There is a great restaurant not too far from here. So, how are you doing kiddo?'

"I'm fine. I can't wait to get out of here.

Maka rejoined them.

"So, where are we going to dinner?"

"Italian," Alan announced.

"Perfect."

The three of them left the facility for the restaurant.

As Alan drove, Maka took the opportunity to share with them what happened with Hurd. She wanted to ensure them they would be safer now. They would probably only have to give a statement now that he was dead. If they had to testify, their testimony would be limited.

Aiyana asked, "Have you found Dakota?"

Maka paused for a moment, she didn't want to share the findings at the cemetery with them. "No sweetie. Not yet. Believe me, my team and I are still working on it. I go back to South Dakota tomorrow."

"Did anything happen from those photos we went through the other night?"

"Yes, you helped a lot. Thank you. I can't talk about the details yet; it was very helpful. I wanted you both to know that it's all going to be OK. Aiyana, I talked to your case workers, and they are helping to facilitate your grants and school. Alan has something to share."

"I made a few calls and was able to get you into USC this winter session. It was too late for fall, but your counselor agreed starting after the holidays would be better. You can stay in the dorm if you want."

"I can leave the shelter?"

"Is it that bad?"

"I don't understand what they are telling me to do."

"What do you mean?

"Their traditional way for counseling, I don't understand it. It's not like our ways."

Aiyana was feeling a little culture shock being away from the reservation. Their ways were different. She was confused, they communicated differently, and their beliefs were different than what she was taught.

"So, you feel you can't relate to their method of counseling?

"Yeah, I don't even know what they are saying."

"There is another organization I can reach out to that might be more helpful to you. There is help out there, we just need to find the right fit for you. Everyone's healing path is different."

Aiyana was glad to hear she could leave the shelter. She wanted to get on with her life and put what happened behind her.

"They want me to change my name. I don't want to."

"Sweetie, I agree with them. It is the only way to keep your third-party information safe and you should consider it while being away from the Reservation, but you have to request it. Some of the people who hurt you were police officers who have access to your social security, driver's license, and things they could keep and have access to. They also have access to databases that can find you. We want to keep you safe. Follow what your counselor and case worker tell you. You can always call me if you need help. Alan and I will check in and make sure it is all being taken care of, you need to stay on top of it too, though."

"I will."

"If you want, Alan said he would love to take you for breakfast or lunch whenever you feel you need a break."

"Thank you. I would like that."

"My pleasure, you can call anytime. I am not far."

Aiyana became very quiet; she stared out the window. Several minutes passed, and Maka wondered what happened.

"Aiyana, everything OK?"

She hesitated for a moment and then started to play with her finger-nails. Maka noticed she was getting fidgety.

"You can tell me."

Aiyana looked up at her, her eyes seemed a little teary.

"What about the other girls that need help, too? I want to help them. I mean, what would have happened to me if you didn't find me? If my brother didn't come looking for me? So many girls don't have that."

She fought back the tears. Aiyana went on to say "I met them. I know them. I have seen things I never believed could happen. How can a human being treat any living being with so much evil?"

This sent a chill down Maka's spine, her body turned into chill bumps, and every hair stood up. She knew Aiyana was right. She knew because it happened to her sister, and it could have happened to her. They paused for a moment.

"Oh, sweetie. I want to help them too. We can pray for them, and I promise I will do what I can to help as many as I can. The best way for you to fight is to learn and use your voice."

"Promise?" Aiyana looked her in the eyes. Maka felt as if she were looking in a mirror at a younger version of herself and part of her sister. She knew she needed to shift the energy. But how do you move from something so deep, so heavy, and pretend that it doesn't exist? How do you go off to dinner and try and forget those young girls left in Tijuana, malnourished, being abused, drugged, and mistreated? She knew they would not forget about them, but to take a moment to clear themselves and be grateful for the moment they could share and regain the strength to help fight for those girls that needed her.

They pulled into the parking lot of La Vecchia.

"Let's leave all this behind us and enjoy a nice dinner. We can talk about this again later. Would that be OK?"

"I think that would be a good idea," Alan said.

"Me too," Aiyana said as she released her seatbelt.

"This is one of my favorite little neighborhood restaurants. I hope you like it."

Alan got out of the car and opened the doors for both Aiyana and Maka. He extended his arms to each of them, as they walked in together.

Wikčémna Núŋpa Šaglógaŋ
28

It was night, the room was lit with a couple of candles on each side of the bed. Maka and Alan lay in bed, heads resting on pillows, holding hands. Only the flickering light from the candles illuminated her soft, glowing skin. He could see the reflection of the flame from one of the candles in her eyes, drawing him in deeper.

Alan knew he was in love with her, but he couldn't always read Maka's energy. She still had her walls up, making it challenging for him to read her. What he didn't know was that she was thinking the same thing he was. She found herself in unfamiliar territory, she hadn't ever fallen in love like this before. At first, it was calming, and soothing to stare into one another's souls. The longer they held each other's hands they began to feel hot, pulsing blood running through their veins.

Alan raised himself on one elbow, leaning closer to Maka, he gently kissed her forehead, lightly gliding over to kiss one eyelid, then the other. His cheek lightly touched hers, allowing his lips to guide him to hers. Kissing her gently, tasting her tongue, her legs started to shake. Alan could feel her tremble, almost shiver as if she were cold.

He whispered, "Maka, are you cold?"

She whispered back, "Not at all."

The way he said her name was like a song whispered to her soul, and her heart beat faster knowing she was safe in his arms. They made love most of the night, connecting in ways they both had only dreamt about. They stayed up talking, having those moments you dream of until they both drifted off to sleep. Not long after they fell asleep the alarm sounded. Maka's laid gently on Alan's chest fast asleep. They both moved slowly to turn off the alarm, staying embraced in each other's arms.

"I can't believe it's already morning."

She jumped up playfully with Alan, straddled him, and softly brushed her inner thigh over his groin, he started to get excited. She ended up sitting on his legs. Alan laughed as she teased him, he had not seen this playful side of her. He liked it.

"You are full of surprise aren't you, Agent Mahpiya?"

They played for a bit, rolling around in bed, laughing, enjoying the moment. The alarm went off again.

"Oy vey," Maka slapped it off.

"I can't believe it's been three days already. Don't go. Can you get re-assigned to an office here?"

"I have to go back. Please understand."

Maka spooned him from behind and wrapped her arms around him.

"You said that you could split your time, and maybe sometimes I can too. I know it won't be easy, but it won't be forever."

"What can I say to convince you to change your mind?"

"Alan…Have you not heard anything I have been telling you?" Maka turned over and looked at him. "I'm sorry. Doesn't all this ever get to you?"

Alan looked confused. "All what?"

"The glamour, the facades, nothing is real anymore. It's the wild west out there again, just more modern. Except this time they don't care about color or your beliefs. It's every person out for him or herself."

"I know." He sat up, turned, kissed her forehead, and slid out of bed. As he started to walk out of the room, he asked, "But I have to chose my battles carefully so I don't lose myself. There is an overwhelming amount of distractions. This is a conversation for a later time." Kissing her on the forehead. Coffee?"

"Yes, please."

She lay in bed, staring at the ceiling for a moment after he left, lost in thought and her morning prayer.

Maka eventually joined Alan in the kitchen, he poured her a cup of coffee.

"Thanks." She leaned against the counter.

"I wanted to tell you how proud of you I am. I have been thinking, what you are doing is important. You are shining a much-needed light of accountability on a very dark topic."

"I didn't see myself as someone who brought things to light that the public wasn't aware of."

They stood in silence gazing into each other's eyes.

"This isn't getting easier. I want you to know I support you."

"Thank you. I want to support you too. I know it's not easy. I don't want to leave you. For the first time in many years, I feel at home with someone, with you."

"Me too."

Maka's phone altered her to several messages coming through, breaking their gaze. Maka looked at the clock on the microwave.

"We better head to the airport. I'm running late."

Maka set her cup in the sink, and looked at her phone.

"Would it be horrible if you missed your flight?" Alan smiled and tried to make a joke.

"Not for us, but for my job." They hugged a moment before he helped carry her bag.

Their drive to the airport was mostly in silence, Alan didn't let go of her hand for a moment. He looked over as she was distracted by her phone. It clicked for him in that moment, *she is her job. Or maybe it's not a job for her but her purpose, much like writing is for me.*

"You're so quiet." Maka looked over at him.

"I was thinking."

"About?"

"Too much," he grinned. "Us, Paythan, all of it. It's been a surreal few weeks."

"I agree. It has been."

"I was thinking about the stories I want to write. I want to write about things with deeper meaning, to help make a difference through my work. Paythan opened my eyes and showed me a different perspective. His journey has forever impacted my life."

There was a bit of a line at the departure area, he didn't mind taking his time.

"You can just pull over here."

"OK." He reluctantly stopped the car; he got out and ran around to open her door.

He didn't want to let her go; they stood outside the airport. He placed his hand softly against her cheek, "Won't you reconsider? Stay." She kissed him, then pulled away "I'm going to be late for my flight."

"Oh, wait. I have something for you."

Alan reached into the car and handed her a large manila envelope sealed shut.

"What's this?"

"Reading material for your flight. Please read it. I love you, call me when you land."

A man and woman were watching them say goodbye, Alan saw them staring. He looked at the couple.

"Isn't she just the most beautiful woman? I'm the luckiest man, I'm going to marry her."

Maka heard part of what he said, and she blushed. The couple smiled and the woman looked at her husband as if to say, why don't you say that about me?

He jumped in the front of his car, and she looked over the envelope and put it in her carry-on. He watched her walk into the terminal and stayed until the doors closed behind her.

Finally, on the plane, she was bumped to first class, and the flight attendant asked if she would like something to drink.

"Sprite please, no ice."

She moved her carry on and saw the envelope sticking out. Slowly, she took it out of her bag and opened it, 8 x 11 paper, two brass ring paper fasteners bound it together. She flipped it over. There was a big pink post-it note in the center of the page. Alan wrote "I miss you already. This is dedicated to all the women who have been victims, all those who survived, and those still missing. To you, for dedicating your life to protecting them and saving them. I love you. We will make this work."

Her eyes teared up, and she sat there a moment, lost in thought, thinking to herself she could still feel his touch. The flight attendant brought her drink and placed it in front of her, breaking her daydream.

"Oh, thank you."

She studied the note for a minute longer, noticing there was something written under it, and peeled it slowly from the paper. This revealed a title page, *PAYTHAN*. Under the title was *Synopsis*. She flipped the page and began to read.

The plane began to ascend. There was a flood of emotions and thoughts that came over her as the plane took flight. The last few weeks flashed through her mind. She thought to herself, *This is what Paythan dreamed of doing through his work.* She remembered an earlier conversation she had with Alan and Aiyana about Paythan. He wanted to bring awareness through his writing and movies to make a change. She realized, even though he physically wasn't here with us, his spirit and message were.

In Memory of
Christopher Knopf

Kim, Miranda and Jahzara

References
Help Is Available

Suicide and Crisis Life Line
- 988
- 988lifeline.org

MMIW:
Coalition to Stop Violence Against Native Women
- www.csvanw.org/mmiw

SWIWC
- www.swiwc.org

Human Trafficking
- 1-888-373-7888

National Human Trafficking Hotline
- humantraffickinghotline.org

SAFE PLACE for Youth:
Someplace To Go. Someplace to Help.
- www.nationalsafeplace.org

National Center for Missing and Exploited Children
- www.missingkids.org

Polaris Project
- polarisproject.org

Mirror Dog Foundation
- www.mirrordog.com

New Lakota Dictionary Online

NLD Online v.5. (n.d.). © Lakota Language Consortium, LLF.
https://nldo.lakotadictionary.org